CONNECTICUT BOXING

THE FIGHTS, THE FIGHTERS AND THE FIGHT GAME

MARK ALLEN BAKER

Published by The History Press
Charleston, SC
www.historypress.com

Unless otherwise noted, all images are courtesy of the author.

Front cover, top left: Bat Battalino. *Courtesy of Rick Kaletsky*; *top center*: Marlon Starling. *Author photo*; *top right*: Gene Tunney. *Courtesy of Library of Congress*; *bottom*: Brian Vera vs. Andy Lee. *Courtesy of Emily Harney/Fightography ©.*
Back cover, top right: New London Club ticket. *Author photo*; *bottom right*: Willie Pep. *Author photo*; *bottom*: members of the Connecticut Boxing Hall of Fame along with host Randy Gordon. *Author photo*.

First published 2021

Manufactured in the United States

ISBN 9781467148085

Library of Congress Control Number: 2021931142

Notice: The information in this book is true and complete to the best of our knowledge. It is offered without guarantee on the part of the author or The History Press. The author and The History Press disclaim all liability in connection with the use of this book.

Friendship is the hardest thing in the world to explain. It's not something you learn in school. But if you haven't learned the meaning of friendship, you really haven't learned anything.

—Muhammad Ali

For my Connecticut friends of the sweet science.

In memory of my dear friend Vikki LaMotta (1930–2005).

CONTENTS

PREFACE

Life comes in three-minute intervals in New England, or at least that's how many fans of the sweet science feel about living in Connecticut. Rich in boxing history, the state draws champions like bees to honey. Attracted by the best gymnasiums with their talented trainers and managers, boxers can craft their skills and gain the exposure they need to take them to the next level. That's because the best promoters and matchmakers in the country are conducting business at the finest venues in the United States—right here in Connecticut. And, when fighters finally reach that next level of performance, they encounter first-class ring announcers, judges, timekeepers, referees, administrators and physicians. A grand presentation in the Nutmeg State, as everyone associated with the sport understands, attracts media attention coast-to-coast and creates opportunities never dreamed possible. Skilled commentators, analysts, broadcasters, newspaper columnists, authors and boxing experts then place participants into proper historical context. Performances are gauged against surnames such as Tunney, Delaney, Kaplan, Battalino, Pep (Papaleo), Duke (Gallucci), Ortega and Starling. While that might not be fair, if you are going to do battle in Connecticut, you better bring your "A" game, as they say, and you damn well better be vertical at the final gong. Nuf ced!

So, just how has Connecticut managed to do it? Well, you are about to find out. Holding the distinction of being the only person to serve the International Boxing Hall of Fame as an author, historian, chairperson, sponsor, volunteer and biographer, not to mention as a member of the

Board of Directors of the Connecticut Boxing Hall of Fame, I felt it was my obligation to uncover the secrets behind the state's rich boxing history. *Connecticut Boxing: The Fighters, the Fights and the Fight Game*, details the fascinating people, places and things that have made this state great. For my twenty-fourth book, and seventh boxing title, I am honored to be given this tremendous opportunity.

ACKNOWLEDGEMENTS

I wish to extend my gratitude to the entire Arcadia/The History Press production team, which always does a magnificent job preparing a title. Also, I offer my genuine appreciation to Michael G. Kinsella, Rick Delaney and Dani McGrath for supporting my work.

As with my previous boxing titles, I have had the opportunity to work with some outstanding institutions, including the International Boxing Hall of Fame, the Library of Congress and the Connecticut Boxing Hall of Fame. A special note of recognition to the following individuals: Ed Brophy, Jeff Brophy, Sherman Cain, Johnny Callas, Glenn Feldman, Emily Harney (Emily Harney/Fightography), Steve Ike, Rick Kaletsky, John Laudati, Gaspar Ortega, Willie Pep (1922–2006), Jim Risley, Marlon Starling, Don Trella and Roger Zotti.

A bulk of professional boxing in Connecticut falls into the hands of two world-class resorts: Foxwoods Resort and Casino in Mashantucket and Mohegan Sun Casino and Resort in Uncasville. Speaking on behalf of every boxing fan, I offer my heartfelt appreciation for your commitment to the sweet science.

As always, my love to my friends and family, especially my wife, Alison.

Introduction

AGAINST ALL ODDS, OR PERHAPS WITH THEM

With its over 5,500 square miles, the Crown Colony of Connecticut was admitted to the Union on January 9, 1788. (It had become a state in July 1776 after agreeing to the Declaration of Independence.) On that very day, the *Times* of London, England, was less concerned about the independent minds of a small group of rebellious colonists across an enormous expanse of water than matters at home. There were priorities. The national newspaper was reporting details regarding the middleweight boxing championship of England being held at Odiham. The contest between Daniel Mendoza and Richard Humphries promised to be well worth the price of admission of half a guinea a head. And, as it turned out, it was. It may have taken the skilled Humphries (Humphreys) almost half an hour to defeat Mendoza, but he did just that.[1]

Knowing the disfavor created by reporting on the contest, the *Times* was certain to publish a disclaimer under the heading "Anti-boxing" just below the account on page three: "As a medium of public communication, we are obliged, in conformity with the usage of other papers, to adopt every opportunity of conveying information to that public, from which we have, since our commencement, received such generous support: otherwise the brutal, though fashionable custom of boxing, should never once have been mentioned in this paper."[2]

As Humphries quelled the defenses of Mendoza, so, too, the British army would eventually defeat the mutinous colonists. Or, so it was hoped. Conflict will forever have an air of uncertainty.

The art of self-defense was carried across the Atlantic Ocean and on to the soil of Connecticut, where it was used to solve disagreements and to entertain. The state's rich history of pugilism would commence—delicately, mind you—ever cognizant of the legality of the sport, not to mention public perception. The first boxing rules, called the Broughton's Rules, were introduced by champion Jack Broughton in England back in 1743, followed by the London Prize Rules (revised 1853) and, later, the Marquess of Queensberry Rules (1867). America, although independently minded, adopted them as well.

Throughout the early twentieth century, boxing continued to struggle to achieve legitimacy, due to the lack of organization and safety of its participants. The sport made its Olympic debut at the 1904 Games in St Louis, and as only Americans participated, they also took home all the medals. While this may have softened public opinion, state regulation—and even that of certain cities, such as Hartford—became the middle ground between outright prohibition and unfettered legalization. For example, the New York State legislature passed the Frawley Act, which permitted professional boxing from August 29, 1911, until November 14, 1917. However, it was repealed. The Walker Law, adopted on March 25, 1920, once again legalized professional boxing in New York State. Two key organizations were founded at this time: a public organization, the National Boxing Association (NBA), and a governmental entity, the New York State Athletic Commission (NYSAC). Both set the course for the sport, and as New York State went, so did others, including Connecticut.

Saturday, October 1, 1921, marked the inauguration of the new Connecticut State Athletic Commission. And for the first time in the history of the state, boxing matches could be legally held within its limits. As a result, boxing flourished. Surnames such as Delaney, Kaplan, Battalino and Pep became household references not only in New England but also across America. But—and there was always a *but* in boxing—the turbulence the sport encountered in the 1960s led to both professional and amateur boxing being outlawed in 1965 by act of the Connecticut State General Assembly. The impact of the legislation was enormous. It not only shattered interest in Connecticut boxing, but it also likely destroyed half a generation's worth of future participants.

Thanks to the efforts of many individuals, the legality of pugilism was eventually restored. The first license to promote boxing in Connecticut since the sport was reinstated was given to longtime advocate Manny Leibert of West Hartford on February 22, 1973. Resurrection, as many understood, would be an enormous undertaking, but it had to begin somewhere. True to form, Connecticut need only look in the mirror to find all the necessary pieces to accomplish the task.

Meanwhile, New York State, having essentially dominated the sport since 1925, threw up the sponge in 1975 and surrendered to casino boxing. Connecticut, mindful of the transition in the sport, not to mention coping with its own set of problems, weathered the storm well in the 1980s. However, it, too, would soon face the same economic factors as had New York.

Now what? Enter Foxwoods Resort and Casino in Mashantucket and Mohegan Sun Casino and Resort in Uncasville. Boxing in Connecticut had found a solution—and not just any alternative, but world-class facilities that attracted premier talent. Seconds out! Connecticut was about to write a new chapter in its rich pugilistic history.

As for the future of the sweet science in Connecticut, boxing has always walked a fine line, be it ethical, legal, medical, moral, racial or regulatory, and that will no doubt continue. The sport has enjoyed a history of consensual immunity from the ordinary law of disorder, based primarily on its social utility—a factor that should never be overlooked. However, that immunity has always been both fragile and cyclical. With this understanding in mind, boxing in Connecticut couldn't be, as you will soon realize, in finer hands.

Chapter One

CONNECTICUT, A PLACE TO CALL HOME

GENE TUNNEY

I did six years of planning to win the championship from Jack Dempsey.
—Gene Tunney

As heavyweight boxing champion through most of the Roaring Twenties, William Harrison "Jack" Dempsey, with his killer instinct and movie-star looks, typified an era basking in economic prosperity, not to mention a generation with a distinctive cultural edge. While his aggressive fighting style and exceptional punching power made Dempsey one of the most feared and popular figures in history, it was his image as an unpolished self-made man, born into a poor Irish and Cherokee family from the heart of the Old West, that resonated with Americans. Dempsey was a man's man. That is, you could argue with him about the best rifle, how to rope cattle and how to attract women.

Enter James Joseph Tunney, who put Dempsey's style under a magnifying glass to discover how to counter its strengths and challenge its weaknesses. In addition, if that meant sparring with some of Dempsey's past opponents, so be it. Equally as handsome, Tunney had a physique to match. He learned to fight in the streets before taking his professional skills and refining them in the United States Marine Corps. Gene was one of seven children and the eldest son of Irish immigrants; the family settled in New York City. His studious mindset was quickly labeled "aloof," especially in contrast to Dempsey, the "Manassa Mauler." Tunney was a gentleman's confidant, the type of guy you could take to the country club and babble about good scotch, the plays of Eugene O'Neill or how to use your 2-iron.[3]

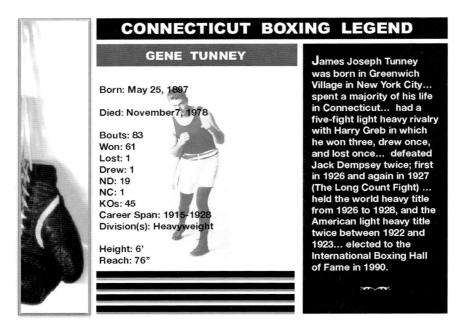

CONNECTICUT BOXING LEGEND

GENE TUNNEY

Born: May 25, 1897

Died: November 7, 1978

Bouts: 83
Won: 61
Lost: 1
Drew: 1
ND: 19
NC: 1
KOs: 45
Career Span: 1915-1928
Division(s): Heavyweight

Height: 6'
Reach: 76"

James Joseph Tunney was born in Greenwich Village in New York City... spent a majority of his life in Connecticut... had a five-fight light heavy rivalry with Harry Greb in which he won three, drew once, and lost once... defeated Jack Dempsey twice; first in 1926 and again in 1927 (The Long Count Fight) ... held the world heavy title from 1926 to 1928, and the American light heavy title twice between 1922 and 1923... elected to the International Boxing Hall of Fame in 1990.

Gene Tunney was inducted into the Connecticut Boxing Hall of Fame in 2008.

More than eighty ring battles into his professional career, Gene Tunney defeated Jack Dempsey—not once, but twice: first, to capture the title in 1926; and again, in its defense, the following year. The second engagement became one of the most famous—and controversial—bouts in boxing history. When Tunney was knocked down in the seventh round, the referee's count was delayed due to Dempsey's failure to go to and remain in a neutral corner. Whether this "long count" in truth affected the outcome remains a subject of debate. But its label has never been questioned. The dual titanic clashes captivated a nation and thrust two of the greatest athletes into the spotlight. In 1928, following a second successful heavyweight title defense (against Tom Heeney inside Yankee Stadium), Tunney surprisingly decided to retire as an undefeated champion.[4]

DESPITE BEING A HEARTTHROB, Tunney, unlike Dempsey, cherished his private life. Shortly before he won the heavyweight title in one of the most stunning upsets in boxing history, he met a striking woman by the name of Mary Josephine Rowland "Polly" Lauder.[5] The champion was smitten by her beauty and charm.

Born into the Lauder Greenway family—her billionaire grandfather was George Lauder, first cousin and business partner of industrialist Andrew Carnegie—Polly was a graduate from the Lenox School in New York and the Finch School of New York and Versailles. Having grown up in a world of wealth and privilege in Greenwich, Connecticut, she never dreamt about falling in love with a pugilist. Prizefighting, as everyone understood, was a taboo. But Gene Tunney was no ordinary prizefighter, and his love for Polly eclipsed all proscriptions, even the ring.

Ironically, the couple's romance turned into one of the most sensational love stories of the 1920s. In August 1928, the lovers' engagement hit many of the newspapers. Their marriage contract was front-page news across the country and touched off a media frenzy—every reporter and photographer sought the first glimpse of the stunning couple. Tunney, as discreetly as a champion prizefighter could be, sailed for England. Polly followed a month later, and the pair was discreetly married in Rome, Italy, on October 3, 1928.[6]

Following their marriage and extended honeymoon, the couple returned to the United States and moved into a historic colonial home in North Stamford. The house, which dated to 1742, required a bit of restoration, but the newlyweds welcomed the challenge. Known as Star Meadow Farm, the property spanned over two hundred scenic acres. There, they raised three sons and a daughter: Gene L. Tunney, John Varick Tunney, Jonathan Tunney and Joan Tunney (Cook).

Gene Tunney spent about a half century in Connecticut. Although he never fought professionally in the state, he felt it was the perfect setting to raise his family. And it always felt like home. Having developed a voracious appetite for classic literature, which was a bit unusual for a prizefighter, Tunney especially enjoyed the works of William Shakespeare. And, further from the norm, he lectured on the bard of Avon at Yale and even befriended George Bernard Shaw, Thornton Wilder, Ernest Hemingway and other writers. Literature was a passion, and Tunney took advantage of every opportunity he had to nurture the ardor. From attending lectures in New Haven to discovering a bookshop in New London, the former pugilist's appetite for the written word was insatiable.

As a businessman, Tunney commuted by train to his office at 52 Vanderbilt Avenue in Manhattan five days a week; his office was a stone's throw from Grand Central Terminal. He sat on the board of numerous companies, including McCandless Corporation, Eversharp Corporation, Pittston Company, Brown Paper and Pulp Company and the Kinzua Lumber Company.

Although he had little to do with boxing after he retired, he was put in charge of the U.S. Navy's physical training program during World War II. It was his friend James Forrestal, then undersecretary of the navy (1940), who convinced Tunney he was needed. The former pugilist was reluctant, understandably so, as he was a major in the Marine Corps reserve. It was an enormous task, yet he accepted the role and performed magnificently. In recognition of his effort, the navy promoted him to the rank of commander.

Tunney, until his death on November 7, 1978, at the age of eighty-one, advocated for the creation of a state pension program to aid professional pugilists. In his plan, 3 percent of the receipts from all boxing contests would be subtracted before taxes to fund such a program. It was a suggestion from a man of conviction, a Connecticut visionary and humanitarian.

Gene Tunney suffered his only loss at the hands of elite boxer Harry Greb. It occurred during his first defense of the light heavyweight championship.

Tunney's Connecticut boxing links are the following: Dan Florio, one of his trainers, also worked with Bat Battalino (Hartford) and Jack Delaney (Bridgeport); his managers Billy Roche and Sammy Kelly (1919–20) also worked with pugilist Dan Murphy (Waterbury); and his elite manager, William "Billy" Gibson, also handled Louis "Kid" Kaplan (Meriden).

Although Tunney's post-career ring appearances were rare, they did take place. On July 11, 1938, he refereed a controversial fight at the Arena in New Haven between George Fitch and Steve Carr. And, on September 17, 1938, he refereed three welter contests during the annual Connecticut amateur boxing championship held at Capitol Park. (Willie Pep had a bye in the flyweight class.)

James Joseph "Gene" Tunney died at Greenwich Hospital in Greenwich, Connecticut, and was interred at Long Ridge Union Cemetery, 154 Erskine Road, in Stamford, Connecticut. Also interred at Long Ridge are author Eugene Blake, actor Alan Bunce, voice actor Kenny Delmar, musician and bandleader Benny Goodman, actress Gilda Radner Wilder and journalist Walter "Red" Smith.

Chapter Two

BRIDGEPORT'S BRIGHT EYES

JACK DELANEY

In reference to Leo Flynn's story regards his battler Eddie O'Hare, I would like to say I have a Bridgeport boy, Jack Delaney, whom I guarantee to knock the daylights out of Eddie O'Hare or any middleweight that Leo Flynn has in his stable.[7]
—*William McPherson, manager of Jack Delaney*

As a youngster, Canadian-born Ovila Chapdelaine, aka Jack Delaney, moved with his family to New England and eventually settled in Bridgeport, Connecticut. Fighting under a variety of monikers as a teenager, including Pat Delaney, he turned pro in 1919. By June 1920, people were beginning to take notice of Bridgeport's "Kayo Kid," thanks to the efforts of his manager, William "Mac" McPherson and, later, Al Jennings.

In his first battle of 1921, early in his career, middleweight Jack Delaney knocked out Boston's "Battling" Silveria in the ninth round of a ten-round scheduled contest at the National Athletic Club in Providence, Rhode Island. Manager Jennings, smelling opportunity, believed it was only a matter of time—and a short one at that—before Delaney would have the scalp of renowned Bridgeport boxer Lou Bogash. Meanwhile, most pugilistic pundits believed that Jennings needed some fresh air. Nevertheless, everyone quickly found out where Delaney stood as a boxer when he tackled Massachusetts middleweight Tommy Robson on April 13, 1921, at Marieville Gardens in North Providence.

Noting the battle, the *Bridgeport Telegram* reported: "From all accounts Jack Delaney got the worst end of the deal in Providence on Wednesday night in his bout with Tommy Robson. The referee gave it to Robson but the fans

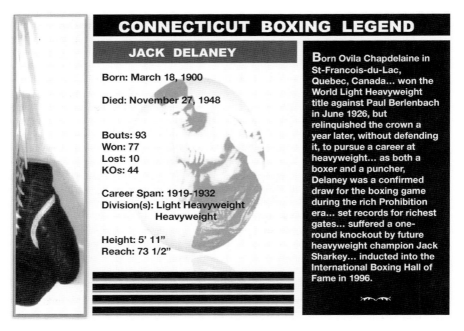

CONNECTICUT BOXING LEGEND

JACK DELANEY

Born: March 18, 1900

Died: November 27, 1948

Bouts: 93
Won: 77
Lost: 10
KOs: 44

Career Span: 1919-1932
Division(s): Light Heavyweight
            Heavyweight

Height: 5' 11"
Reach: 73 1/2"

Born Ovila Chapdelaine in St-Francois-du-Lac, Quebec, Canada... won the World Light Heavyweight title against Paul Berlenbach in June 1926, but relinquished the crown a year later, without defending it, to pursue a career at heavyweight... as both a boxer and a puncher, Delaney was a confirmed draw for the boxing game during the rich Prohibition era... set records for richest gates... suffered a one-round knockout by future heavyweight champion Jack Sharkey... inducted into the International Boxing Hall of Fame in 1996.

Jack Delaney was inducted into the Connecticut Boxing Hall of Fame in 2008.

gave it to Delaney who is known as Pat [the boxer also fought under Pat Delaney] in that burg."[8]

However, the *Telegram* also reported that the *Providence Journal* stated: "Delaney won the scrap—won it from here to Bridgeport in the opinion of a great majority of the customers. His manager Al Jennings, climbed into the ring at the finish of the combat and started to harangue the blood-thirsty fans but his flow of eloquence was rudely interrupted, the majesty of the law in the person of Officer Lake descending upon him and shooing him out."[9]

Although Delaney recently drew veteran Jack McCarron, who had over 150 bouts under his belt, many felt the aspiring Tommy Robson was a far greater challenge. Disposing of his next two challengers, Delaney landed himself on his first major undercard. On July 25, 1921, he knocked out Bert Colima (37-3-5) of Los Angeles after one minute and thirty-seven seconds of fighting in the seventh round. The scheduled eight-round contest took place at Ebbets Field in Brooklyn. In the main event of the evening, Pete Herman regained the world's bantamweight championship by taking a fifteen-round victory over Joe Lynch.

Under the headline "Saturday Marks Beginning of Legalized Boxing in the State," the *Bridgeport Telegram* reminded fight fans:

> *Saturday, October first, will mark the inauguration of the new state athletic commission and for the first time in the history of Connecticut, boxing matches may be legally held within its limits… Many experienced sporting men of the state believe that the boxing game is in danger of strangulation because of the new regulation which prevent bouts being held on holidays, forbid the taking of motion pictures, and the extra expense caused by the licensing of managers, seconds, and preliminary boxers, who from the small amount of work which they will get hardly afford the expense.*[10]

The Ebbets Field victory ignited Delaney, who posted six consecutive victories before turning to Jackie Clark in his first fight of 1922. With over 150 bouts behind him, Clark made the ten-round distance against his rival, but it was close. The crafty veteran was staggered in the sixth, nearly out in the eighth and dazed again in the ninth round. In the end, it was Delaney in a points victory.

On January 27, 1922, Delaney dropped Jack McCarron three times on the way to a points victory. The rematch win, in Bridgeport, was precisely what Delaney needed at this point in his career. Taking a closer look, the *Telegram* reported: "Delaney dropped McCarron to the count of nine in the ninth round with a crashing right to the jaw. A left to the stomach and a right to the head sent McCarron to the floor for the count of four in the final canto. He displayed his gameness by sticking the round but was floored again for the count of nine by the local battler."[11]

Finally, it was time for the bout that all of Bridgeport has been waiting for: Jack Delaney versus Lou Bogash. Everybody around town was talking about it, wondering: Could the Bridgeport youngster defeat the Bridgeport boxing legend who had nearly four times the level of experience? The popular pair would meet on February 13, 1922, at (State Street) Casino Hall in Bridgeport. The prices for seats were scaled at two dollars for general admission, three dollars for reserve and five dollars for ringside. Suffice it to say, it was the "hottest" ticket in town.

THE BATTLE OF BRIDGEPORT

The hype surrounding the conflict began building about a month prior to the engagement. Lou Bogash (Luigi Boccasio, also Luigi Buccassi), aka the "Blond Italian," opened his preliminary training for the contest on January 10 over at the Acorn Club. His preparation was six days ahead of his opponent.

Calm, cool and collected, the veteran sparred a bit, played a couple games of handball and shadowboxed. Delaney, who planned on opening his camp over at the Columbia Athletic Club (AC), was also relaxed and sanguine.

Both fighters, understanding the gravity of their Bridgeport contest, had engaged in warm-up battles. Bogash took a four-round TKO victory over Brooklyn boxer Young Hickey, while Delaney put away the aforementioned McCarron. In a reminder, the *Bridgeport Telegram* noted: "The Bogash-Delaney battle will go fifteen rounds. It will be the longest fight in Delaney's career. He has not yet fought over twelve rounds. Both boxers are due to rake off 25 percent of the house."[12]

As far as loyalty was concerned, Bridgeport was split between both fighters, Rhode Island favored Delaney and both New York and Boston favored Bogash. In terms of weight, Bogash hoped to enter the ring at 152 pounds, while Delaney figured to tip at 158. Rumors flew from both camps. Fearing that their fight strategies might be leaked to the press, both factions released only the information they wanted known. Bogash, who had never punched harder, was also working on a new right-hand punch and improved footwork. Delaney brought in Joe Woods, another New Yorker pugilist with excellent speed, to improve his reaction time. On to the fight.

The result was crisp and clear, even if the reviews were mixed: Bridgeport had a new ring idol, and his name was Jack Delaney. According to the *Hartford Courant*: "He [Delaney] won the title after he and Bogash had sidestepped, waltzed and did various other things inside the arena tonight. But one of those things wasn't fight. There was very little of that during the forty-five minutes the pair were inside the ropes. Delaney was too good for Bogash the way the latter fought tonight."[13]

As the newspaper saw it, Bogash made far too many mistakes.

The blond Italian outgeneraled himself in that he waited until the latter rounds of the scrap before he resorted to those tearing in and slugging tactics that have won him previous battles. Bogash merely cantered through the first seven rounds and Delaney jabbed and right hooked his way to a comfortable lead. It was not until the ninth that critics gave Bogash a round. In that session the Italian took the offensive and he landed his left and right with telling frequency upon Delaney's chin and nose.[14]

Let's look at the final rounds. Having taken the tenth, Delaney slowed enough in the eleventh to allow Bogash to land ample combinations and body punches to take the round. The twelfth was even, and the thirteenth, at least to some, proved the best round of the contest. Both boxers unleashed unrelenting volleys that had the crowd on their feet. However, the round appeared too close to call. The fourteenth saw Bogash, with little choice, take the offensive. Landing two hard lefts, he drew blood from Delaney's mouth and nose. Bogash needed the final round, and Delaney knew it. "Bright Eyes" shut his adversary down by not allowing him inside. In the end, Delaney's defensive skills proved far superior; his height and reach advantage allowed him to effectively use his left hand to ward off his rival. Granted, Bogash was a difficult target in that famous crouch of his, but you can't win fights if you can't land punches. And Bogash could not. The Casino drew a record crowd, to say nothing of a gate of just under $10,000. For the remainder of 1922, Delaney would post a record of 4-2. But it was clearly a turning point for the fighter.

Aftermath

As for the talented Bogash, nothing short of a sensational boxer, he battled until 1931. Following his loss to Delaney, he picked up victories over Mickey Walker, Tommy Loughran and "Panama" Joe Gans and even managed to go the twelve-round distance against Harry Greb, with the *New York Times* giving the newspaper decision to Bogash.

In 1923, Jack Delaney would compile a record of 5-0, with one no contest, and he even battled at the Polo Grounds. The following year, he fought thirteen times and notched a record of 10-2-0 and 1 no contest. In his first appearance at Madison Square Garden, Delaney knocked down Paul Berlenbach three times on the way to a knockout victory.

In his breakout year, 1925, Jack Delaney fought ten times to a record of 7-2-1. Losing to Paul Berlenbach in front of twenty-three thousand fans in the new Madison Square Garden (III) in a bout for the world light heavyweight title was hard to swallow, or accept, if you will, yet Delaney did exactly that. Delaney, who floored Berlenbach in the fourth, had him groggy in the

When "Bright Eyes" Jack Delaney had his first clash with former AAU wrestling champion Paul Berlenbach, the 1924 fight was billed as "The Wrestler versus The Boxer."

sixth and seventh, saw his New York antagonist rally back and win (7 to 6, with two rounds even) by a razor-thin margin. Thankfully for the Bridgeport boxer, he was able to avenge his loss to Berlenbach the following year and capture the NYSAC world light heavyweight crown, moreover, via a fifteen-round unanimous decision.

Chapter Three

MERIDEN MUSCLE IN HANOVER PARK

LOUIS "KID" KAPLAN

Located at the "Crossroads of Connecticut," a mere two hours from New York City and Boston, the city of Meriden, known for its over 3,000 acres of municipally owned park space and 74 different recreational areas, attracts visitors from all across New England.
—City of Meriden

As evidenced by a population growth of over 12 percent during the previous decade, Meriden, with its 27,265 residents, had become a noted manufacturing center in 1910. Underlying this increase was silver, a precious, shiny, grayish-white metal that could be transformed and used in a variety of ways.[15] Due to the large number of silver manufacturers forming in or relocating to the city, including the Meriden Britannia Company (a predecessor of the International Silver Company), the municipality quickly earned a new moniker, "Silver City." And, where there was work, there was also discretionary dollars and leisure time.

On May 30, 1894, Memorial Day, a beautiful piece of property called Hanover Park, located on Hanover Pond, a man-made body of water, opened in Meriden. Over the years, the property was used for many things and called many names, perhaps the most familiar that of Camp Tyler. During the Civil War, a battalion of artillery and cavalry (Company B) was stationed on the land. Later, ownership fell primarily to the Meriden Electric Railway Company. Drawing pleasure-seekers from around the region, Hanover Park was transformed into a recreation center, casino, theater and

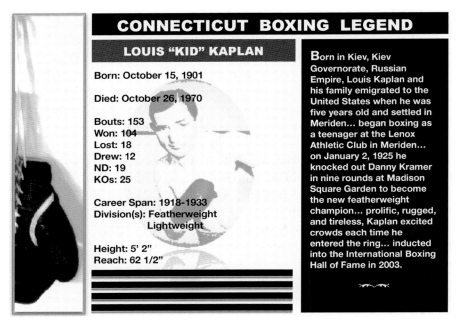

CONNECTICUT BOXING LEGEND

LOUIS "KID" KAPLAN

Born: October 15, 1901

Died: October 26, 1970

Bouts: 153
Won: 104
Lost: 18
Drew: 12
ND: 19
KOs: 25

Career Span: 1918-1933
Division(s): Featherweight
Lightweight

Height: 5' 2"
Reach: 62 1/2"

Born in Kiev, Kiev Governorate, Russian Empire, Louis Kaplan and his family emigrated to the United States when he was five years old and settled in Meriden... began boxing as a teenager at the Lenox Athletic Club in Meriden... on January 2, 1925 he knocked out Danny Kramer in nine rounds at Madison Square Garden to become the new featherweight champion... prolific, rugged, and tireless, Kaplan excited crowds each time he entered the ring... inducted into the International Boxing Hall of Fame in 2003.

Louis "Kid" Kaplan was inducted into the Connecticut Boxing Hall of Fame in 2005.

amusement park all rolled into one. The picturesque setting soon became a popular destination.

As the *Hartford Courant* commented: "That the Meriden people appreciate the park is evident from the crowds there every day attending the league games in the afternoon, or packing the theater in the evening, enjoying the antics of the minstrels, or in the dancing pavilion waltzing and eating ice cream."[16]

Routinely drawing over one thousand daily visitors, the park also became a social center, a place to observe and be seen. The open-air theater, with its covered roof, provided diverse entertainment, from vaudeville to opera. The *Courant* continued: "Situated as the park is, between Meriden and Wallingford, a great many people from the latter town constantly visit it. Picnic parties from all over the state make it their camping ground, and lodges and societies go there on their outings. A favorite place with these kids is the photograph gallery just west of the merry-go-round, where for the modest sum of 25 cents one may secure four tintypes."[17]

Ironically, paralleling interest in the park was also that of the fight game. This was perhaps no better stated than by the *Hartford Courant* under the headline "Local Boxing Game Never More Popular":

It would not take a pair of opera glasses to enable the sport followers of this city and vicinity to dope out the fact that the boxing game in and around Hartford is at its greatest height of popularity right now. The 2,000 people who centered from all directions at East Hartford Wednesday night, and packed Comstock Hall tighter than that building was ever packed before, is a little bit more than circumstantial evidence that such is the case. The game has been tried and found guilty of being extremely popular.[18]

What was becoming clear, as early as 1916, was the need for larger pugilistic venues. As Connecticut searched for a boxing mecca, East Hartford was trying to fit the bill, as was Manchester, Windsor Locks and New Britain. But no single solution had been found.

From 1916 until 1922 (no fights were held in 1918 or 1921), Hanover Park became the summer (June until September) home for boxing—typically twenty-nine rounds of milling supplied by three or four bouts—conducted under the auspices of the Lenox Athletic Club. Weather permitting, the event often drew over one thousand spectators. Connecticut boxers who battled included the following: Ansonia's Pinky Silverberg; Bridgeport's Pete August, John Credon, Johnny Mason and Young Hogan; Hartford's "Kid" Delucca, "Battling" Green, Gaylor Lewis, Frankie Mack, "Kid" Marto, Neil McCabe, Chick McCormick, Joe Rocco and Sammy Waltz; Meriden's Charley Brown, Jimmy Jenkins, Charlie Pilkington, Willie Rose, Kid Tusse, Joe Wanic, Jimmy Welton, Young Attell and Young Mack; New Haven's Charley Bergen, Chick Brown, Joe Currie, Mickey Doherty, Jimmy Proto, Tommy Shea and Mickey Travers; New Britain's Frankie Burns; New London's Dave Palitz; Norwalk's "Battling" Kunz; Wallingford's Tracey Ferguson; and Waterbury's Johnny Moroney, Young Rocco and Johnny Shugrue. The out-of-state participants were as follows: Massachusetts's Dick Barry; New Jersey's Johnny Drummie; New York's Johnny Bedell, Dutch Brandt, "KO" Jasse, "Battling" Lahn, Phil Lundy, Billy Meyers, Young Russell and Frankie Wilson; Ohio's Young Oscar Gardner; Pennsylvania's "Battling" Reddy; and Rhode Island's Al Wiltse. And making the journey from Canada were Eddie Tremblay and Red Vigeant.

Likely the best contest held at Hanover Park, prior to 1920, took place on July 21, 1919. The headline in the *Hartford Courant* told the story: "Waltz Gains the Edge over Shea, Forces New Haven Boy to Protect Himself in Fifteenth to Avoid Knockout." The paper reported: "Sammy Waltz, the Hartford scrapper, annexed the featherweight championship of New England at Hanover Park here tonight when he whipped Tommy Shea of New Haven

Kaplan's first appearance on a Hanover Park boxing card happened on August 14, 1920, against the familiar face of Mickey Travers. The New Haven fighter had already defeated Kaplan twice.

in convincing style before 3,000 fans. The crowd taxed the capacity of both the bleachers and grandstand and also surged around the ring. All the tickets were disposed of way before the main bout was scheduled to go on and at least 200 were doomed to disappointment."[19]

From a matchmaking perspective, Waltz, with a record of 25-14-5, looked even against Shea, who had a record of 29-15-12. But Shea had lost four of his last six battles, while Waltz had won four of his. While the *Courant* clearly had Waltz dominating the event, the *Meridan Morning Record* saw the fight as a draw—such was the era of no decision.

The *Courant* continued: "Waltz was practically the aggressor throughout the fifteen rounds, being credited with the first seven rounds in which he piled up a commanding lead with the eighth honors about even. For the remainder of the fight Waltz altered his tactics and had Shea hanging on in the last round to stave off defeat by the knockout route."

Hanover Park got its first taste of local phenom Louis "Kid" Kaplan on August 14, 1920. The Meriden boxer, with a record of 10-4-3, was on an undercard and facing New Haven's Mickey Travers (14-5-6). Far from being strangers to each other, Kaplan had already lost to Travers twice, in two consecutive battles, the first a ten-rounder at the Arena in New Haven, and the second a six-rounder at the Auditorium in Waterbury. To the delight of the fans, both pugilists went toe-to-toe in their eight-round draw at the park.

Kaplan's first headliner contest at Hanover Park came on August 10, 1922. With a record of 36-9-8, the Meriden fighter was now far from an undercard talent, and it showed. He easily defeated Philadelphia's Eddie Wagner (45-6-10) to capture a twelve-round points victory. This was an important conquest, as Kaplan avenged the loss suffered at the mitts of Wagner back on June 9 at City Hall Auditorium in Meriden. And it confirmed that Kaplan's talent was as genuine as his popularity.

Even though many knew that the festivities of September 14, 1922, would draw from near and far, they didn't know to what degree. Nearly seven thousand spectators came from all across New England to witness Kid Kaplan (37-9-8) tackle Waterbury's Johnny Shugrue (40-9-5) at Hanover Park. Every artery in and around Meriden was packed with fans of all ages headed to the front gate of the venue. Chaos ensued when women began fainting due to the heat and congestion.

Quickly transcending that of a sporting event, the enticing four-bout card, fought under the auspices of the Hanover Athletic Club, was mirroring more of a social, if not historic, phenomenon. Twenty-two rounds' worth of preliminaries opened the event, highlighted by a ten-round draw between Wallingford's Tracy Ferguson and Bridgeport's Pete August. With anticipation high, the main event turned out to be nothing short of a classic battle from beginning to end. With Kaplan taking the early rounds, his opponent, part of the popular Shugrue fighting family, had little choice but to take the middle sessions.[20] By the tenth, Kaplan, aware that he had to finish strong to win the fight, did exactly that.

The *Hartford Courant* saw the early rounds like this:

> *Kaplan knocked Shugrue down with a left hook to the jaw in the first round and a minute later Shugrue knocked Kaplan down with a right to the jaw. Both regained their feet in a jiffy. Kaplan's terrific offensive gave him the first round and the second was even. Kaplan showered Shugrue with rights and lefts to the face and body in the third round and easily won that session. Shugrue started shooting rights to the head in this round. In the fourth Kaplan again knocked Shugrue down, the Waterbury boy bounding off the mat after a shower of typical Kaplan blows to the head. He was up in an instant and fought back hard, but the round went to the Meriden pride.[21]*

Although the fifth was even, you could sense a bit of momentum shift. Shugrue altered his punch strategy, turning first to a left hook to the body, followed by a right hook to the head. And it worked. Although Kaplan may have been conserving energy for a big finish, he started losing rounds. The shot of the night, at least from Shugrue's perspective, was a powerful left

In 1922, Kid Kaplan defeated Eddie Wagner and Johnny Shugrue in back-to-back appearances in Hanover Park. Both of his opponents had over forty career victories.

hook to Kaplan's jaw that lifted him off his feet. But the iron-chinned "Kid" took it before beginning his closing argument.

The *Courant* continued: "He [Kaplan] knocked Shugrue down in the eleventh with a left hook to the jaw and in the twelfth he had everything his own way, the Waterbury lad apparently being tired after the twelve furious rounds."[22]

The contest was awarded to Kaplan. Afterward, Denny "Dinny" McMahon, the fighter's manager, claimed the junior lightweight championship of New England on behalf of his Meriden meal ticket. Interest in the park declined following the fight. Later, it took on renewed interest as a popular swimming spot. Unfortunately, pollution from industrial factories along the river eventually prompted the beach's closure. The Meriden resort was eventually converted into a parking lot for buses.

Today, visitors to the Hanover Pond Linear Trail in Meriden can get a sense of what it was once like by using their imagination. Enhanced by an informative kiosk, one can almost picture the excitement created by the park. But it will never replace one of the most exciting evenings in the history of Meriden, courtesy of Louis "Kid" Kaplan.

Chapter Four

THE EPIC RISE

CHRISTOPHER "BAT" BATTALINO

You know what a champion is? A champion is someone who's ready when the gong rings—not just before, not just after—but when it rings.
—*Jack Dempsey*

Back in 1925, the Park Street Casino was one of the premier places to witness amateur boxing in Hartford. From Eddie Barnett (state amateur featherweight champion) and Billie Cunningham, to Cy Ackerman and Bat Battalino, they were all there. Each whet their skills, showcased their wares and were optimistic about a future in the fight game. Battalino, like others, also participated in the amateur shows held Monday nights at Capitol Park, over on Wethersfield Avenue, all part of an informal boxing circuit. Not yet a headliner but not far from it, Battalino was among a "rising crop" of talented Hartford fighters.[23] For example, when the Olympic Athletic Club conducted a ten-bout promotion on Tuesday evening, November 3, 1925, at Foot Guard Hall, the three main features were Noah Kaplan ("Kid" Kaplan's Brother) versus Bill Cunningham, "Bat" Battalino (Hartford) versus Johnny Mack (New Haven) and Joe Howard (Hartford) versus "KO" Jack Jaffe (navy champ.). Not bad for the seventy-five cents it cost for general admission.[24]

Christopher Battalino, born on February 18, 1908, was the son of Carminuccio "Carmen" Battalino (Battaglia, 1868–1939) and Maria Domenica "Amelia" Marrese (Battalino, 1883–1967), an Italian immigrant family living in Hartford, Connecticut.[25] His handsome frame was topped with thick brown hair, and his brown eyes matched his tinted complexion. He attended Brown School on Market Street until the fifth grade. Education

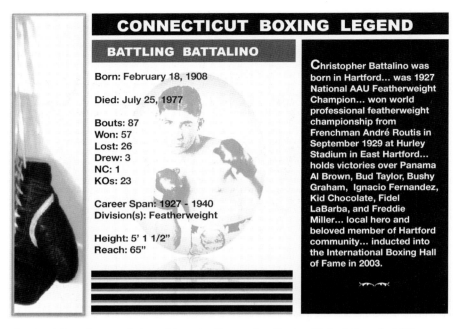

CONNECTICUT BOXING LEGEND

BATTLING BATTALINO

Born: February 18, 1908

Died: July 25, 1977

Bouts: 87
Won: 57
Lost: 26
Drew: 3
NC: 1
KOs: 23

Career Span: 1927 - 1940
Division(s): Featherweight

Height: 5' 1 1/2"
Reach: 65"

Christopher Battalino was born in Hartford... was 1927 National AAU Featherweight Champion... won world professional featherweight championship from Frenchman André Routis in September 1929 at Hurley Stadium in East Hartford... holds victories over Panama Al Brown, Bud Taylor, Bushy Graham, Ignacio Fernandez, Kid Chocolate, Fidel LaBarba, and Freddie Miller... local hero and beloved member of Hartford community... inducted into the International Boxing Hall of Fame in 2003.

"Battling" Battalino was inducted into the Connecticut Boxing Hall of Fame in 2005.

served its purpose, but the family's needs came first.[26] Similar to some children, Battalino never attended high school, opting instead to labor in Connecticut's generous tobacco fields. He was a stout five feet, six inches, and weighed 126 pounds, and the work kept him in shape, even if it wasn't easy. Certainly, or so he believed, there must be alternatives. And there was. Hartford was a hotbed for amateur pugilists, no better exemplified than by Russian immigrant Louis "Kid" Kaplan.

The youngster embraced the sport, and people took notice. One of them happened to be Ed Hurley, matchmaker for the Olympic Athletic Club.[27] Nobody seemed to know the Connecticut fight game better than Hurley, who routinely traveled the state looking for talent. In addition to his interest in fighters such as Fritz Adamson (New Haven), Joe Bard (Hartford), Joe Brown (New Haven's impressive AAU middleweight), Jimmy Clinch (New Britain, one of the few who ever dropped Battalino), Billy Flynn (New Haven), Joe Howard (Hartford), Noah Kaplan (Meriden), Jackie Kelly (Waterbury), Johnny Mack, Andy Murry (New Haven), Tony Starr (Glastonbury), Joe Triano (New Haven) and Duke Vaughn (New Haven), he also liked Battalino.

By the summer of 1926, Battalino, having garnered the amateur featherweight championship of Connecticut, was grabbing headlines in the sports section of the *Hartford Courant*: "'Bat' Battalino Knocks Out Holyoke Boy in 1st Round."[28] It was during a competitive boxing card at Capitol Park, on the evening of July 26, 1926, that boxer Armand Massey, of Holyoke, made the journey south to Hartford to catch a short left hook to the chin a mere two minutes into his conflict against Battalino. Carrying the moniker "Hartford Bearcat," Battalino simply dominated the 126-pound class. Later that summer, he moved up to 129 pounds.

On December 26, 1926, Christopher "Bat" Battalino received a special gift for the holiday season. He was featured, along with other "State and Hartford 1926 Champs and Leaders," in a full-page collage of photographs that appeared in the *Hartford Courant*. Others noted included Elmwood Endees, City Amateur Champions (baseball); Dixies, Hartford Basketball Champions; Connecticut Aggies Basketball Five, New England Title Claimants; Victor Hopkins, Motorpaced Champion of America, who starred in Hartford Velodrome; Ken Reid, Farmington Country Club, state junior golf champion; Frank Ross, Hartford Sequin Golf Club, Connecticut Amateur Champion; Johnny Sill, Wethersfield Country Club, Hartford District Golf Champion; Al Conley, New London, Connecticut's lightweight champion; Jack Delaney of Bridgeport, world's light heavyweight champion; Mike Esposito of Stamford, state bantamweight champion; and Joe Howard, Hartford Boy Connecticut Middleweight Amateur Champion. An athletic club's dream come true, Battalino, who had become enormously popular, was basically fighting as often as he wished.

Taking a look at the amateur champions around the state of Connecticut entering 1927. Hartford had three: Joe Howard at 160 pounds, Battalino at 126 and Ray Strong at 118. New Haven, another amateur fighting stronghold, had Nick Florentino at 105, Pete Florentino at 112, Fritz Adamson at 147 and Duke Vaughn at 175 pounds and up. Finally, Meriden had John Krock at 135. It was simply an amazing time for Connecticut boxing.

So, just how popular had Bat Battalino become? Some of the advertising for Thursday-night boxing at Foot Guard Hall included only one surname: "BATTALINO."[29] When he was on the card, every inch inside the hall was occupied by fight fans. Even the aisles needed to be cleared before the doors of the place, which closed at 8:30, could be shut. Fans were routinely pushed away from the door while begging for admittance. Battalino's approach was simple: At the gong for the opening round, attack your opponent and overwhelm him with enough artillery to bring down a battalion. Advancing constantly, he would not relent. If his antagonist survived, which was a big *if*, he repeated the performance in the second round. Battalino showed no fear; even when he was hit on that iron chin of his, he would not wince. Shows at the Foot Guard Hall typically ended between 10:30 and 10:45 p.m. Afterward, some of the fans would mill about on High Street, smoking a cigarette while decompressing from the action. A few hoped to catch a glimpse of the handsome Italian ring idol or perhaps even pat him on the back in affirmation of a quality performance. Folks absolutely loved Bat.

By the spring of 1927, Battalino had become a knockout artist. His success forced matchmakers such as Ed Hurley to forage New England, looking for anybody who could put Battalino to the test. When Hurley discovered a Boston lad named Jack McCormick, with a record of three knockouts in fifty seconds, he believed he had found the ideal opponent. Arranging shows for the Massasoit AC at Foot Guard Hall, Hurley inked the Hub fighter to a match with Battalino on Thursday, March 24, 1927. Increasingly unfazed by any hype from Hurley's mouth, Battalino entered the ring and transmitted a death scowl to referee Frankie Portelle—even Frankie knew he was going home early. As the opening bell sounded, Battalino cocked his right hand then proceeded to drop McCormick three times, with three solid rights to the chin, leaving Portelle little choice but to stop the bout. McCormick was out on his feet. And, in his very next battle, on April 1, out in New Britain at the new T.A.B. Hall, Battalino stopped Jack Miller of Lawrence, Massachusetts, in thirty-five seconds. Miller was down twice, only seconds after the opening gong, and his handlers threw in the towel. Battalino wasn't only defeating his antagonists; he was humiliating them.

Hurley's last attempt, for all intents and purposes, to find a suitable assassin—I mean opponent—for Battalino was Andy Callahan, also from Lawrence, who happened to be a New England champion. If anyone could find a flaw in Battalino's armor, or so Hurley was certain, it would be the Irish southpaw. After all, the power-punching Callahan created a stir when he knocked out Frankie Erne, former New England champion, in a recent tournament. On April 15, it took Battalino two minutes and thirty seconds to drop his antagonist. Face-down on the canvas, Callahan needed to be carried back to his corner and revived.

To little surprise—if, of course, you were from Connecticut—on April 26, 1927, Christopher "Bat" Battalino, nineteen years old, captured the national amateur championship in the featherweight class (126 pounds). It was in typical Battalino style: an opening-round knockout of Louis New of Milwaukee. Sending New to the canvas twice in the first minute, Bat put on a convincing demonstration.[30]

A Hero's Welcome

Despite a pouring rain, over three thousand fans gathered at Union Station on April 27 to welcome home Christopher Battalino. As the train from Boston pulled in a bit after 7:00 p.m., fans, some of whom had waited for over an hour, cheered for the pugilist as they raised him to their shoulders and carried him to a waiting automobile. Joining him in the vehicle were his manager, Hy Miller, his trainer, Lenny Marello, and members of a welcoming committee. The crowd, many carrying red torchlights, next led a parade that included a police car, a band and the champion's vehicle up Asylum Street. The parade proceeded from Asylum to High Street, then on to North Main. From there, it was over to Sheldon, then along Front Street, or Battalino's neighborhood, where fans cheered and waved both Italian and American flags. Finally, it reached Battalino's home at 514 Front Street.[31] It was all the police could do to escort the fighter up the stairs and into his home.

Welcoming their son, Bat's parents were a bit stunned by the celebration. It seemed as if the entire neighborhood had somehow managed to squeeze their way into the family residence. Also greeting the champion was his sweetheart, Lillian Rotondo. Following the short family visit, Bat was carried off to the Charter Oak Athletic Club on Windsor Street for another "meet and greet." It was quite a day for the youngster, who was utterly exhausted by the time the festivities drew to a close.

On May 11, 1927, Battalino was the star attraction at an amateur show that opened the outdoor season of the Velodrome in East Hartford. Eight consecutive knockouts—four as part of the national championship—along with a prestigious title, can transform even a local pugilist into a main attraction. Paul Ventura of Lawrence, Massachusetts, accomplished what few had when they met the "Hartford Bearcat" in the ring: he made it to the second round. Yet, there would be no celebration on his part. Using his trademark right, Battalino hit his mark, his antagonist's chin, and dropped Ventura to his knees. Instinctively, Ventura quickly staggered to his feet, only to realize that he should have taken a count. Seeing Battalino reloading in the viewfinder, he panicked and dropped to his knees without being hit. As such, he was disqualified, and Battalino was awarded a second-round TKO (technical knockout). Days later, in a rematch at the same venue, it took the Hartford phenom only forty-seven seconds to knock out Ventura.

Unquestionably, Battalino had fought his way out of the amateur ranks. It was only a matter of time before he was mentally ready to make the jump to professional boxing. His shows had outgrown Foot Guard Hall and were drawing large crowds, more than six thousand at the Velodrome (the venue had a capacity of 20,000). His final fight as an amateur came on May 27, 1927, at the Velodrome, against Philadelphia gladiator Jimmy Walker. Battalino floored his opponent five times—three times in the first round, twice in the next—on the way to a second-round TKO.

TURNING PROFESSIONAL

On June 6, 1927, Christopher "Bat" Battalino (125½ pounds) made his professional debut against New Yorker Archie Rosenberg (126 pounds) at the Velodrome in Hartford. An impressive crowd of over four thousand fight fans turned out on a Monday evening to watch their hometown protagonist knock out his New York adversary in the second round. Rosenberg, who possessed a sharp left hook, had replaced Otto Goldberg, who could not make weight. Battalino, in what looked like a slip, did go to one knee during the bout. Rosenberg was dropped in the second to a five count by a Battalino right hand. Sensing the kill, the Hartford fighter landed a right to his opponent's jaw that sent him horizontal. Somehow, Rosenberg was on his feet as the count hit ten. Referee Henry Gerrity gave him the benefit of the doubt, and the fight briefly continued. Battalino then unleashed an uppercut that sent Rosenberg down for the final time.

Posting a record of 7-0-2, with one no decision (exhibition) for the year 1927, Battalino appeared satisfied; he never fought outside the state of Connecticut. His quickest victory was a first-round knockout over Rhode Island pugilist Jimmy Rossi. New Haven's Tony DePalma was the first professional opponent to go the distance (six rounds) against Battalino (the Hartford fighter took the decision). New York's Joe Curry was the first professional opponent Battalino faced with over thirty victories. He was also the first to battle Battalino to a draw and to meet him in back-to-back contests. The Hartford boxer went 1-0-1 against Curry. Battalino suffered his first major injury, a fractured left hand, during his second battle against Curry.

In his first full year as a professional boxer, Battalino posted a record of 6-1, against five different opponents. Of the five boxers he faced, New York featherweight Milton Cohen, a one-time bantam contender, was by far the best. Yet, Battalino defeated him twice in decision victories. Schenectady boxer Johnny Ciccone, with a losing record, became the second fighter Battalino faced in back-to-back contests and was the first boxer to defeat the Hartford pugilist.

In a travesty of truth, Battalino, ahead on the referee's scorecard, lost the decision on April 3, 1928. Arbiter Jack Watson declared Johnny Ciccone the winner of the bout despite the figures on his own tally sheet. After being consulted, Commissioner Thomas A. Donahue, who just happened to be attending the bout, stood behind Watson's decision. It was simply an injustice. By June, the fighter had faced additional injury—he hurt his eyes (also in a battle with Ciccone), was sick and had his arm in a cast—and was forced to refuse over half a dozen matches.

Bat Battalino's breakout year came in 1929. Posting a record of 6-0 (three decisions and three knockouts), he faced six different opponents, including one elite fighter ("Panama" Al Brown), and fought for the world featherweight title against Frenchman Andre Routis. Fighting only in the state of Connecticut, he fought three times in Foot Guard Hall, twice in Bulkeley Stadium and his championship bout in Hurley Stadium.[32]

Training over at Charter Oaks gymnasium, Battalino was dropping holiday weight to make 125 pounds for his first contest against New Yorker Ralph Nischo. Not much was anticipated from Nischo, and not much was given, as the fighter was knocked out in the first round on January 4.

Moving on to the familiar face of Joe Curry on February 7, Battalino, having drawn and defeated the fighter earlier in his career, dropped him with a tremendous right cross to the left cheek in the second round.

A veteran out of Florida, Tony Leto was next to face Battalino on February 21. Although the Hartford fighter hoped it would be a short contest, he also knew better. Leto, who had won eleven consecutive ring battles, hadn't lost since May of the previous year (1928).[33] The fight was stopped after two minutes of the seventh round, when referee Billy Conway examined a gash over Leto's left eye and felt it was too dangerous for the contest to continue. Leto, who hit the canvas multiple times, managed to drop Battalino late in the second round, and honestly, the Hartford fighter was lucky the bell saved him. More than happy to capture victory in one of the toughest battles he had faced in months, Bat, with his cut eye and injured hand, pocketed the win and headed home. Meanwhile, Hy Malley booked his meal ticket, along with some of his boys, for an exhibition on May 16. In addition to Battalino, Malley's stable included Frankie Angela, Pat Diaz, Mickey Flahive, Zeke Mazer, Art Pollowitzer and Young Portell.

On Monday, April 29, 1929, Christopher Battalino married Lillian Rotondo at St. Anthony's Church. On that same day, Battalino was presented with a medal from Mayor Walter E. Batterson for the bravery he exhibited in saving a child from the waters of the Park River only a few weeks before.[34]

Christopher, age twenty-two, and his Italian wife, Lillian, nineteen, quickly established a home on Woodbridge Street in Hartford.[35]

Waterbury's Eddie Lord, a seasoned veteran who typically won three times as many bouts as he lost, met Bat Battalino inside Bulkeley Stadium on June 5. The bout was billed as for the featherweight (126 pounds) championship of Connecticut. The hype for the fight attracted over 5,500 fight fans to the venue—not a bad draw, considering it rained during most of the undercard. Tickets were scaled at $1.05, $2.10 and $3.15. It wasn't a walk in Bushnell Park, but Battalino managed to win seven of the ten rounds to grab the victory. And he nearly had Lord out in the sixth term when he floored him to a nine count; it was the only knockdown in the fight. On the downside, Battalino injured his hand in the fourth round and used that powerful right of his to carry him to victory. The injury would take at least until July to heal.

Word was that if Battalino put on a strong showing against Lord, he would meet Andre Routis, the world featherweight champion. In a sign that this really might be the case, Joe Jacobs, who managed the champion, found his way to Hartford to trade jabs with Ed Hurley, who would likely promote the bout.[36] Also, Jess McMahon, the crafty New York promoter and matchmaker who was thinking about a New Haven battle between the winner of this contest and Kid Chocolate made it to Hartford. Making it even more interesting, "Dinny" McMahon, Kid Kaplan's manager, had recently purchased Lord's contract.

However, before Battalino (17-1-2) could even begin thinking about Routis, he had to test his mitts; specifically, his left hand. Malley, following considerable negotiation, landed him a bout against, of all people, the aggressive "Panama" Al Brown (59-7-6) at 125 pounds. One could certainly question Malley's choice: If Battalino needed a test, this was it. Brown, bantamweight champion of the world, would not have his crown at stake. It proved to be a prudent judgment on the part of the Panama-born fighter, as Battalino took eight of ten rounds to capture the decision.

WITH LESS THAN THREE years of professional boxing experience behind him, Christopher Battalino (124½ pounds) captured the world featherweight title by defeating Andre Routis (126 pounds) in a fifteen-round duel. It happened at Hurley Stadium on September 23, 1929.

The twenty-one-year-old American stunned and at the same time satisfied a hometown crowd estimated at fourteen thousand by dancing around the twenty-nine-year-old Frenchman as if he had both feet stuck in the sand. The

A mature, yet forever imposing, Bat Battalino takes time to strike a familiar pose. *Courtesy of Rick Kaletsky.*

performance by Routis confused some. Could this have been the same French feather who had defeated elite boxer Tony Canzoneri by a split decision only the year before? Or was it just that Battalino, with his speed, accuracy and ring generalship, was truly that good? It appeared to be the latter.

From evading nearly every attempt by Routis to mount an attack, to even controlling him at close quarters, Hartford's own dominated the scoring. Using his powerful left, Battalino went hard to the body of his adversary but struggled to find an angle to reach the chin. To his credit, Routis, who guarded his chin like a prisoner, was never in retreat, but nor was he forcing the fighting. Although the Frenchman could land at short range, his long artillery was so far off that he looked foolish at times. Despite no clear knockdowns, Battalino was close to delivering his rival in the fourth round. This was courtesy of a volley of combinations; consequently, Battalino bruised both of his hands. In the sixth, Battalino caught a wild hook while he was off balance, and it sent him to the canvas without a count. It may have been a slip; it was simply too hard to tell. If the American had a weakness, it was his inability to penetrate the defense of Routis. The Frenchman never let his guard down.[37]

From his professional debut against Archie Rosenberg at the Velodrome, to his featherweight title fight against Andre Routis at Hurley Stadium, 841 days had passed, or two years, three months and 18 days, including the end date. To capture an undergraduate degree in pugilism in under four years was a rarity, but such was the epic rise of Christopher "Bat" Battalino.[38]

Chapter Five

"WILL-O'-THE-WISP"

WILLIE PEP

After you're the champion, first you lose your legs, then you lose your reflexes, and then you lose your friends.
—*Willie Pep*

Life is measured by moments, special moments, not by time, as many believe. On July 7, 1995, I spent nearly an entire day in Canastota, New York, with one of the finest pugilists ever and, without question, the greatest featherweight to enter a boxing ring: Guglielmo Papaleo, aka "Willie Pep." With little advanced warning, which was often the case when the elite fighter made the over 230-mile pilgrimage from central Connecticut to central New York, I prepared hours of questions for my final formal interview with the man many knew as "Will-o'-the-Wisp" and "Willie the Wisp," and whom I always knew as my grandfather's favorite fighter. Ed Brophy, the director of the International Boxing Hall of Fame, called me the night before and asked me to host the seventy-two-year-old Pep, and I gladly obliged.

The familiar powder-blue Oldsmobile, Connecticut plates "W*PEP," rolled into the driveway of the Boxing Hall of Fame late morning. Noting the four bumper stickers on the back of the vehicle—"Turn Into A Winner," "Help Cure Paralysis," "Proud to be an American" and a (visit) Rhode Island decal—I planned to ask the relevance of the banners as filler questions, if I needed them. I would not. Sauntering into the museum with that familiar walk of his, Pep greeted everyone in the museum as if he had slept there overnight and was waiting for them. The handful of visiting fans

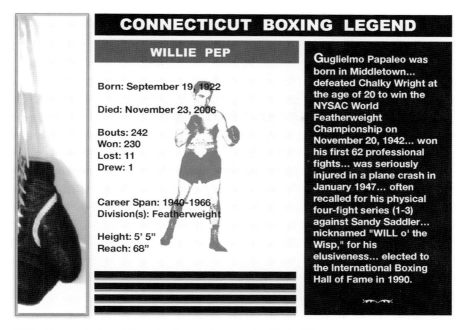

CONNECTICUT BOXING LEGEND

WILLIE PEP

Born: September 19, 1922

Died: November 23, 2006

Bouts: 242
Won: 230
Lost: 11
Drew: 1

Career Span: 1940-1966
Division(s): Featherweight

Height: 5' 5"
Reach: 68"

Guglielmo Papaleo was born in Middletown... defeated Chalky Wright at the age of 20 to win the NYSAC World Featherweight Championship on November 20, 1942... won his first 62 professional fights... was seriously injured in a plane crash in January 1947... often recalled for his physical four-fight series (1-3) against Sandy Saddler... nicknamed "WILL o' the Wisp," for his elusiveness... elected to the International Boxing Hall of Fame in 1990.

Willie Pep was inducted into the Connecticut Boxing Hall of Fame in 2005.

was stunned by the encounter. Once they realized who he was, most felt anointed; moreover, it was as if he fell out of his plaque on the wall and onto the floor and arose to a three count. It was a rare Madison Square Garden moment, 265 miles from 4 Pennsylvania Plaza.

Born on September 19, 1922, in the largely Italian community of Middletown, about sixteen miles from Hartford, Pep was the son of a Sicilian construction worker, Salvatore, and Maria (Marchese) Papaleo. In the late nineteenth and early twentieth centuries, the once predominantly Anglo-Saxon Middletown saw a large number of Irish, then Italian, immigrants arrive to work in area factories and farms. By 1930, the Papaleo family was renting a home in Hartford.

> *Back then you did what ya had to do....* [Willie, who spoke in staccato bursts, never really finished a sentence, his voice simply faded out or he moved on to another comment.] *We shined shoes.... We'd work our corner...everybody had a corner...me and Gallucci, you know Johnny Duke....* [I nodded my head in affirmation, even though at the time I was living in central New York and was not as familiar with Duke as I should have been.] *We did good*

and before long others wanted the corner....Well, we had to defend our ground....We were kids."

Spending over two and a half years crafting his skills as an amateur, the youngster quickly realized he had talent. Pep told me a story he had repeated numerous times over the years.

I started fighting when I was about fifteen...or fifteen and half years old [prompted by a bullying incident]...*making about eight bucks a fight. My old man liked sports and the money I brought home....Down in Norwich, we would fight at this place called the Du-Well* [also Duwell] *Athletic Club. I always gotta kick out of the name....At the time* [1938], *I was the Connecticut amateur flyweight champion....I even won* [claimed] *the Connecticut amateur bantamweight title the following year....Anyway, they would bring in the Salem-Crescent AC* [Athletic Club] *from Harlem, kids, Black kids who could really fight....I saw a really tall kid and asked my manager about him and he said that's the kid you're gonna fight....I told him to be serious, well, he was....I mean I weighed about a hundred pounds and this guy was a featherweight....So I fight the guy and he's all over me, punching, pushing, just swarming me....I mean I was just tryin' to hang in there....When he won, I heard the name Ray Roberts, so I remembered it. Later, I find out it was Sugar Ray Robinson. Even that wasn't his real name.* [Seeing him searching for the name, I said, "Walker Smith."] *Yeah, well the kids don't get paid in New York, so they head to Connecticut where amateurs were allowed to fight for money.*

At five feet, five inches tall, Pep was a solid right-hander, quick afoot, mindful of his opponents. His obscure debut as a professional came against a lackluster opponent—or "tomato can," as they're commonly referred to—on July 30, 1940. Defeating a local kid, Joey Marcus, in a four-round decision at Bulkeley Stadium, Pep was thrilled.[39] It was a victory in his own backyard. Similar to most beginning fighters, he fought locally first before opportunities pushed him farther from home (primarily the Valley Arena in Holyoke). Not leaving New England until November 1941, Pep headed to California for a brief visit. I never understood why, so I asked him.

Well, I was around Hartford, fighting, not very happy, so a couple of wise guys say, "We got this car and were going to go to California."...I went with them, four days and four nights, we were kids, I was young, we got

Willie Pep points out the similarities between his Oldsmobile (*left*) and the Chevrolet (*right*) owned by Ed Brophy, director of the International Boxing Hall of Fame.

there so the first thing I had to do was fight, so we got to the gym, Main Street Gym, I'll never forget it…began training with Manuel Ortiz. He says, "Listen, I'll give you a dollar a round." Great, so I'd hang around and make four dollars and we could all eat.…I finally fought him [Ortiz] *in Boston two or three years later* [July 17, 1944, Braves Field] *and he was a nice fella, nice guy, I really liked him. I got to meet my hero George Raft, but I didn't spend any time with him. Hell, it was a big thing for a kid to meet these guys.*

Called the "Will-o'-the-Wisp" by sportswriters (either Dan Parker of the *Daily Mirror* or Bill Corum of the *Journal American*) for his supreme defensive skills, Pep could sidestep a bullet at sixty feet. A masterful foot soldier, as graceful as some of the finest, he was as astute as a hawk. His first bout at Madison Square Garden came on December 12, 1941, against gadabout boxer Ruby Garcia. Pep took the four-round decision, followed shortly thereafter by his second Garden duel against the experienced Pittsburgh slugger Sammy Parotta. Pep took that four-round verdict as well. Compiling an astonishing record of 54-0 (you read it right), Pep won the world featherweight championship on November 20, 1942. It was a fifteen-round unanimous decision against elite California fighter Albert "Chalky" Wright, a future Hall of Fame stablemate.

I was twenty years old, on the 20th of September [actually September 19, 1922, but close enough], *and I won, won the title, my fifty-fourth straight win, again, my manager put me in with the right guy….* ["Was Wright what you anticipated?"] *Well, Chalky Wright was a puncher. If you stood still, he would hit you and knock you down or knock you out. So, the idea was to move, and I moved fifteen rounds. Not once, twice* [1944], *the third time* [1946] *I knocked him out….* ["Did he fight you any differently the last time?"] *He was a puncher, not a clever boxer…a puncher just comes in and throw punches. He was a smart boxer, but he wasn't clever. He just kept walking in and…when I knocked him out, he came to me and said, "You son of a bitch you punched me in the mouth."…He was a nice man. He was one of the nice guys in the boxing business."*

Pep's implausible consecutive win streak of sixty-two bouts finally came to an end on March 19, 1943, inside Madison Square Garden. His opponent was Sammy Angott, the Cleveland fighter who had retired as undefeated lightweight champion only four months earlier. Making a comeback, Angott (134 pounds) took the ten-round unanimous decision over Pep (130 pounds), the NYSAC world feather champion. Thankfully for the "Wisp"—or, perhaps, wisely—this was not a title bout. Pep was a 3-1 betting favorite. Originally planned for fifteen rounds, NYSAC trimmed the fight out of fear that Pep, if victorious, would have a claim to the lightweight crown. For the feather, it was a money bout. The masterminds behind the Hartford boxer— and there are seldom only a few behind a great fighter—were trainer Bill Gore and manager Lou Viscusi.

About trainer Bill Gore (1892–1975), Willie had this to say:

The guy had to be one of the great trainers of our time, our era….He trained Melio Bettina, Johnny Cesario, Roy Harris….What made him great was he was there all the time….He came to the gym every day, never missed a day….I listened to him, and he made a champ out of me.

About manager Lou Viscusi (June 15, 1909–August 10, 1997):

Viscusi moved to Hartford in 1929 and was around with a couple fighters, that's how I met him….I was only 15 years old….I'm very happy I was at the right spot at the right time. And having a great manager, this guy Viscusi knew my body couldn't take so much punishment. He put me in with the right guys.

On his opponents:

> *When you fight main bouts, you have to pick the right guy. He* [Viscusi]
> *picked guys that were in my category. They might be even a little better
> than me…but they weren't going to beat me up.…He was a great, great
> manager…a brain, new my capabilities more than I knew them myself.…I
> was always in the gym and in pretty good shape. I goofed a couple of times.*

Pep perspicaciously defended his title on an "as-needed basis," once annually, from 1943 to 1947 (twice in 1948), while fighting ten to twelve nontitle bouts each year and serving in both the navy and army in World War II. His successful defenses included a cast of great pugilists: the pride of East Boston, Sal Bartolo (1943, W 15); California's Chalky Wright (1944, W 15); New York's Phil Terranova (1945, W 15); Sal Bartolo, again (1946, KO 12); Flint, Michigan's Jock Leslie (1947, KO 12); and Cuban Humberto Sierra (1948, KO 10).

Fate intervened on January 5, 1947, when the "Wisp" sustained a broken leg, a cracked vertebra and a chest injury in the crash of a chartered plane near Bridgeton, New Jersey, during a snowstorm. Thankfully, he was still alive. Against the odds, he returned to the ring five months later. (Reluctant to bring up the topic, I nevertheless asked him about it when he appeared comfortable with me.)

> *I was coming up from Florida to New York, into Newark.…I was going
> to start training…I was on vacation…and it was raining, snowing and
> thunder, and we're going to land in Newark…and the plane kept circling and
> circling, so finally tried to relax…ya gotta bed down, so I laid back, closed
> my eyes…they were still circling…finally he* [the pilot] *said "we're going
> down and land in a wooded area."…Now there are no wooded areas in New
> Jersey, only houses.…We hit a couple trees and ripped the plane apart, I
> remember I was laying on the floor, on my belly, my back was killing me, my
> leg was killing me, a guy turns me around and says, "Geez, that's Willie Pep,
> how do ya feel?" They put me on a stretcher and brought me to the hospital.
> They put a cast on my chest and cast on my leg.…There* [he pointed to
> the location] *is a little mark there you can see right there, it was broken right
> down there.…Five months later we took the cast off, I was suing the company*
> [he says quietly, twice]…*then right into the gym, I had a fight a month
> later, July* [June 17, 1947 against Victor Flores in Hartford] *and I
> won* [W10]. *I boxed another fifteen years.*

A popular Willie Pep publicity photo noting the awards won by the elite pugilist.

Willie Pep (125 pounds) had been the featherweight champion for nearly six years when he faced Sandy Saddler (124 pounds) of Boston for the first time on October 29, 1948, in a battle at "The Garden." Dropped twice for nine-counts in the third round, Pep took a left hook in the fourth round that sent him down for good. Losing his world featherweight title in his seventh defense was heartbreaking. It would, however, mark the inception of a classic fight saga for both elite fighters, the duet forever linked in ring lore. Worth noting, and not often enough, was that, between his losses to Angott and Saddler, Pep fought over seventy successive bouts without a defeat (only one draw, Jimmy McAllister). In an era when streaks seemed exclusive to baseball and players such as Joe DiMaggio, Pep conducted a period masterpiece.

An esurient Pep regained the featherweight crown from Saddler on February 11, 1949, via a fifteen-round unanimous decision. He would defend the title three times (1949–50) before losing it again to Saddler via eighth-round knockout on September 8, 1950. The rematch, held at the Polo Grounds on September 26, 1951, was Pep's final loss to Saddler. It was confirmation, at least in his own mind, where he then stood as a fighter. It was, by many accounts, one of the dirtiest contests ever fought in a boxing ring. How dirty, you ask? Well, NYSAC revoked Pep's license for seventeen months and suspended Saddler for two months because of their fouling.

> *I like to forget about him* [Saddler].…*He fought me.…I had been around a long time.…I wouldn't say I was finished, but I was slowly getting whipped, and he was in the prime of his life, a good fighter.…He beat me…once he beat me because of my eye, you can't see you can't fight, lost that fight…hurt my shoulder, lost that fight.…First time I fought him he knocked me down three times.…I had fought three guys that had beaten him, before I fought him, so, I thought, I'm going to have no trouble with this guy…he was a tough son of a gun, and he rose to his height when he fought me.…He was skinny and thin, Sandy was a tough guy, he could jab and whack you around.*

An intrepid Pep persevered, fighting until 1959 and continuing his winning ways; he won sixty of sixty-six bouts during that period.

> *Ya know boxing is a funny thing…I got hit a few times, and you get hit a few times, ya know that's the name of the game. If ya don't get hit, they figure something is wrong. I took a few beatings, not beatings, "wackin arounds," a couple guys, Sandy* [Saddler] *banged me around a bit… but not as many as the ordinary guy. I lost eleven fights, five of them*

TKOs [his interpretation], *in those fights, I didn't get hurt I got knocked down and they stopped the fight, which is great, three times you get knocked down and they stop the fight. Sandy knocked me down twice, three times, twice TKO'd me* [Saddler KO'd (definition dependent) Pep three times], *the other guy*[s] *who TKO'd me I forget their names* [Boston's Tommy Collins in 1952, the controversial Lulu Perez in 1954 and Hogan "Kid" Bassey in 1958], *no, I wanna forget their names…* [laughs]*…but still I didn't get hurt, I got knocked out, but listen ya get knocked down, you get back up.…I lost five decisions…those were the tough fights to lose.…I'm perhaps one of the luckiest fighters that ever lived, in the world. Look at me, I survived an airplane crash, the Navy…* [the list continues], *six wives.…The good Lord took care of me.*

Pep attempted a comeback at age forty-four and won nine of ten fights (1965–66)—as if there was something left to prove. When the gloves no longer fit, the official (Hall of Fame) record read: 242 bouts, 230 wins, 11 losses, 1 draw and 65 knockouts.

During the interview, I tried but failed to get Pep to admit that there was anything more to his loss against Lulu Perez at the Garden on February 26, 1954. In his 190th bout, give or take a fight, Pep was eleven years older than Perez and the number-one featherweight contender. The loss made no sense—but perhaps cents—as Perez was a 6-5 favorite the afternoon of the contest before moving to a $3^{1}/_{2}$-1 favorite at the start of the battle. Many bookmakers even took the fight "off the boards," meaning no more bets were taken. Regardless, I took the fighter at his word.

I asked him about another event, on July 25, 1946, in Minneapolis, in the third round of a nontitle bout against Jackie Graves. Constantly in motion, Pep, weaving, bobbing, dodging and dancing, won a round without landing a single solid punch. (He did admit to casting a few light jabs.) Impressing the judges solely with his ring prowess, Pep was masterful. He carried a folded newspaper article attesting to the accomplishment in his wallet and even gave me a copy. For the record, Pep won the fight via knockout in the eighth round.

We talked all day, and I recorded a large part of our conversation—even contributing some of the material to a screenwriter who was working on a movie about Pep. We ate lunch at McDonald's across the street from the boxing shrine and were constantly interrupted by a steady stream of fight fans. We chatted about everybody, and everything, or so it seemed: Steve Belloise, Larry Boardman, Joey Giardello, Rocky Graziano, Tony Janiro, Vikki (a dear friend of mine at the time) and Jake LaMotta, Frankie Ryff and Chico Vejar, to name only a few.

Elected to the International Boxing Hall of Fame in 1990, Pep added that impressive inaugural class asterisk to his biography. As the interview concluded, Willie headed over to Graziano's motel and restaurant just down the street at 409 North Peterboro Street. So revered in the small upstate New York hamlet, the inn had a special room reserved and even named after the "Wisp." Understanding that mediocrity knows nothing higher than itself— to borrow an Arthur Conan Doyle quip—all Pep sought, at least in his final years, was recognition that he had risen above it.

Willie Pep's Greatest Ring Battles

Date	Winner /Result/Round	Loser	Venue/Location
November 20, 1942	Willie Pep, UD 15	Chalky Wright	Madison Square Garden, NY ***
January 29, 1943	Willie Pep, UD 10	Allie Stolz	Madison Square Garden, NY
March 19, 1943	Sammy Angott, UD 10	Willie Pep	Madison Square Garden, NY
April 9, 1943	Willie Pep, SD 10	Sal Bartolo	Boston Garden/ Boston, MA
June 8, 1943	Willie Pep, UD 15	Sal Bartolo	Braves Field, Boston, MA ***
July 7, 1944	Willie Pep, UD 10	Willie Joyce	Comiskey Park, Chicago, IL
July 17, 1944	Willie Pep, UD 10	Manuel Ortiz	Braves Field, Boston, MA
August 4, 1944	Willie Pep, UD 10	Lulu Constantino	Municipal Stadium, Waterbury
September 29, 1944	Willie Pep, UD 15	Chalky Wright	Madison Square Garden, NY ***
June 7, 1946	Willie Pep, KO 12	Sal Bartolo	Madison Square Garden, NY ***
September 10, 1948	Willie Pep, UD 10	Paddy DeMarco	Madison Square Garden, NY
October 29, 1948	Sandy Saddler, KO4	Willie Pep	Madison Square Garden, NY ***
February 11, 1949	Willie Pep, UD 15	Sandy Saddler	Madison Square Garden, NY ***
September 20, 1949	Willie Pep, TKO 7	Eddie Compo	Municipal Stadium, Waterbury ***
March 17, 1950	Willie Pep, UD 15	Ray Famechon	Madison Square Garden, NY ***
September 8, 1950	Sandy Saddler, TKO 8	Willie Pep	Yankee Stadium/ Bronx, NY ***
September 26, 1951	Sandy Saddler, TKO 9	Willie Pep	Polo Grounds, NY ***
	UD = Unanimous Decision	SD = Split Decision	*** Title Fight

A chronological list of "Willie Pep's Greatest Ring Battles."

Chapter Six

THE BELOVED

JOHNNY DUKE

Don't let anything without a heart beat you.
—Sugar Ray Robinson

When you talk Connecticut boxing, a flood of names immediately comes to mind, such as Christopher Battalino, Louis Kaplan, Willie Pep and Marlon Starling. But the name that ignites the greatest emotion seems to always be Johnny Duke. A more beloved man affiliated with the sport of boxing in Connecticut could not be found. To most folks, he was simple "Duke," aka Johnny Duke.

Born Giulio Gallucci on May 18, 1924, on Russell Street in Hartford, he was the son of the late Teresins (Console) Gallucci Nesci and Luigi Gallucci. He was also the stepson of Frank Nesci. The youngest of three brothers, which is never easy, Giulio was part of a poor immigrant Italian family that redefined the meaning of struggle. Deserted by their father, the family had little choice but to turn to community assistance. Quitting school in the sixth grade in order to help his family, Giulio did everything from selling newspapers to shoveling snow. The security of his family came first. And just as important, at least to this youngster, was not disappointing his mother.

Giulio and his buddy Guglielmo Papaleo became bootblacks and pounded the sidewalks of Hartford. Staking claim to their street corners (often Ann and Asylum, or along Front Street) was of prime importance to the youngsters, and if that meant holding their ground against a challenge, then so be it. Toughened by their surroundings, the pair eventually joined a gym

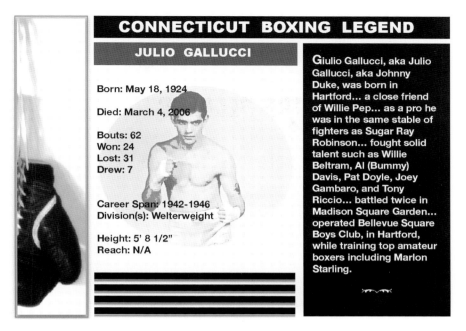

CONNECTICUT BOXING LEGEND

JULIO GALLUCCI

Born: May 18, 1924

Died: March 4, 2006

Bouts: 62
Won: 24
Lost: 31
Drew: 7

Career Span: 1942-1946
Division(s): Welterweight

Height: 5' 8 1/2"
Reach: N/A

Giulio Gallucci, aka Julio Gallucci, aka Johnny Duke, was born in Hartford... a close friend of Willie Pep... as a pro he was in the same stable of fighters as Sugar Ray Robinson... fought solid talent such as Willie Beltram, Al (Bummy) Davis, Pat Doyle, Joey Gambaro, and Tony Riccio... battled twice in Madison Square Garden... operated Bellevue Square Boys Club, in Hartford, while training top amateur boxers including Marlon Starling.

Julio Gallucci, aka Johnny Duke, was inducted into the Connecticut Boxing Hall of Fame in 2005.

and took their defensive skills even further. Altering their ethnic identities, both youngsters, with a bit of encouragement from Judge Jacob Dunn (yes, the boys occasionally went a bit too far), began impressive amateur boxing careers, Guglielmo as "Willie Pep" and Giulio as "Johnny Duke." Later, Gallucci would claim that he earned the nickname "Duke" because he was a sharp dresser—as if the handsome Italian youth, who turned many a female head, needed accessories.

When his buddy Guglielmo made his professional debut on July 25, 1940, in of all places Bulkeley Stadium, well, Giulio simply couldn't believe it. And everyone else he told couldn't believe it, either. But it was true. The main event that evening featured an undefeated Marty Servo, of Schenectady, against a Zivic from Pittsburgh—it didn't matter whether it was Eddie or Fritzie, it was still a Zivic from Pittsburgh, and that meant trouble. But Servo, who happened to be the cousin of Lou Ambers and handled by Al Weill, wasn't too worried. Matchmaker Lou Viscusi liked the card he had assembled, not only for the popular Servo, who had made his headquarters in Hartford the previous summer and created a considerable fan base, but also for Willie Pep.

Sparring with Pep, Giulio learned to box better than he ever imagined. Furthermore, it gave him access to information, such as management, training and punching techniques, that would prove invaluable. Fighting ten times in 1940, Pep was undefeated and making money glove over fist. Granted, there were a few tomato cans in the mix, but Jimmy Ritchie at least had a winning record, and having "Kid" Kaplan as a referee wasn't half bad. So, "Julio Gallucci" (he dropped the alias "Johnny Duke") laced 'em up and got serious—as if entering a ring with Pep wasn't commitment enough.

Making his professional debut on October 5, 1942, Julio Gallucci defeated Boston pugilist Red Luce by way of a TKO in the third round (the bout was scheduled for six). The clash took place in Holyoke, Massachusetts, a hotbed for pugilism. Granted, the Valley Arena wasn't Madison Square Garden, and Red Luce fought more like Red Barber, but it was a start. Posting a record of 3-3-1 in 1942, Gallucci's career was off and running. In 1943, his first full year as a professional, Gallucci compiled a prolific record of 17-10-3, battling out of venues such as Ridgewood Grove, St, Nicholas Arena, Roosevelt Stadium and even Madison Square Garden.

That's right, "The Garden." Gallucci took a four-round points victory over Ray Puig in the second of the four-round openers on April 2, 1943. A lightweight by the name of Ike Williams took the six-rounder that followed— yep, that "Ike Williams." And, no offense to Gallucci, but most fans were there to see the main event. It featured Beau Jack taking an impressive ten-round victory over Henry Armstrong. Doing his best to keep his nerves in check, Gallucci tried to stay focused, tried to pretend that the presence of Mike Jacobs was no big deal and tried hard not to be entranced by the sights, sounds and smells of the Garden. But for a first-time fighter, that was an impossibility. Having moved to Harlem, the nineteen-year-old Gallucci, as luck would have it, landed in the same stable of fighters as Sugar Ray Robinson and was managed by the great George Gainsford. The New York fight scene was exciting, dynamic and ruthless; ergo, a pug could be here today and gone tomorrow. And this despite the impact of World War II.

Fighting about once a week, Gallucci's skills were improving, so much so that on June 11, 1943, he was back in the Garden. Facing upstate fighter Tommy Rotolo (135½ pounds), who was undefeated at 7-0-1, proved to be a bit more challenging than anticipated for Gallucci (140¼ pounds), and he lost the decision. It was the four-round opener to a fabulous feature that saw Henry Armstrong, on the comeback trail, taking a hard-fought ten-round decision over former lightweight champion Sammy Angott. Had the Hartford fighter known it would be his second and final time battling in the

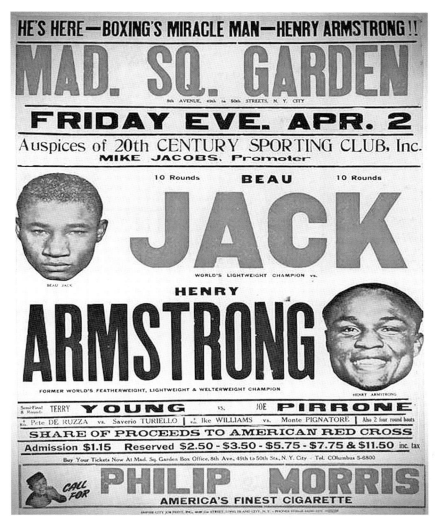

A poster advertising the Madison Square Garden boxing card that would not only be Julio Gallucci's venue debut but also his first victory in the prestigious venue. (His name does not appear on the advertisement.)

prestigious venue, the loss might have bothered him more. But it did not. It was still the Garden on a Henry Armstrong card, in front of thirteen thousand city fight fans.

In 1944, Gallucci went 4-10-1 while facing the likes of Joey Gambaro, Tony Riccio and Al "Bummy" Davis, the latter one of the "hottest" boxers in the fight game. While no loss was fun, being felled with a Davis left hook eight seconds before the end of round two, and at the Arena in New Haven, was a bit tough to swallow. The action left Gallucci thinking long and hard about his future in the fight game. No doubt he was a bit harder on himself than he needed to be, and it took a toll on his confidence. He finished the year with three consecutive losses.

Following the holiday season, Gallucci, having not fought since December 6, 1944, decided it was time for a change. He resurrected his amateur alter ego, Johnny Duke. Battling in both recorded and unrecorded bouts in 1945, while staying close to home, Duke's performance lined his pockets, but not much more. After August 30, 1945, he didn't fight another recorded battle until July 22, 1946.[40] And by the end of August 1946, he had hung up the mitts.

Gallucci tended to his loving wife, Helen, who had also been his childhood sweetheart, and their three beautiful daughters, Diana, Nancy and Helen. Although he was employed by the City of Hartford as an ombudsman for thirty-seven years, Duke didn't find his true calling until he began running the Bellevue Square Boys Club in 1959. The gym, operated by the Police Athletic League, needed a volunteer to run the facility—and not just any participant, but someone who commanded respect. Originally called the Dashaway Club, with its first club in the country located in Hartford back in 1860, the Boys Club formed a national organization in 1906. The group, with its rich history, was about to get even better with the addition of Johnny Duke. Priding himself on dedication and hard work, he always held a full-time job while running the club.

From the Main Street Gym to Bellevue Square, then on to the San Juan Center north of downtown Hartford, Duke directed punch traffic until 2002. After thirty-seven years at Bellevue Square, Duke's gym was closed. The building was demolished—but not Duke's heart, nor the souls of those he touched. He had changed lives. The club, thanks to Duke, quickly emerged as a haven for underprivileged youth and a top spawning ground for amateur and professional boxers.

Duke's expertise assisted in the development of many top-flight amateurs. A teacher's ability has always been mirrored in the success of their students. Here are a few of Duke's.

One of only four Connecticut boxers to win a national Amateur Athletic Union title, James W. "Jimmy" Blythe, a heavyweight, was the AAU titleholder twice (1958 and 1959) and was a regional champion of the Golden Gloves competition three times. In 1961, he worked as a sparring partner for Floyd Patterson, the world heavyweight champion.

A super heavyweight bronze medalist at the 1995 World Amateur Boxing Championships in Berlin, Lawrence M. Clay-Bey not only earned the right to go to the 1996 Summer Olympics in Atlanta but was also named team USA's captain. Turning pro in 1997, he compiled a record of 21-3-1.

Emerging in the early 1970s, Donald L. "Donnie" Nelson competed in the welterweight class and won the New England Golden Gloves Title. Moving on to the Nationals, he lost a heartbreaking close decision to "Sugar" Ray Seales, who just so happened to be the only American boxer to win a gold medal at the 1972 Summer Olympics. Turning professional in 1974, and even winning the vacant USA New England Lightweight crown, Nelson was one of the most promising undefeated fighters in New England before being tragically killed in Hartford.

A prolific southpaw, Mike "Machine Gun" Oliver turned pro in 2001 following a lengthy and successful amateur career. Emerging quickly as a force in the bantam ranks, he collected the USBA super bantam crown (2006–7), the International Boxing Organization (IBO) super bantam title (2007) and the New England state super bantam belt. In 2013, he stepped up in weight and captured the World Boxing Association (WBA)–North American Boxing Association (NABA) U.S. featherweight title.

Winning four straight Western Massachusetts Golden Gloves titles (1985–88) and three consecutive New England Golden Gloves titles (1986–88), John "Iceman" Scully advanced to the championship round of the National Golden Gloves tournament on two occasions. Compiling an amateur record of 57–13 (not including two junior Olympic bouts at age fifteen and two exhibition matches), Scully turned pro in 1988. Assembling an impressive record of 38-11-0, he hung up the gloves in 2001.

Other students of Duke's include the following: Marlon "Magic Man" Starling, the WBA, WBC and Lineal Welterweight World Champion; Herbie Cox, a former five-time Connecticut amateur boxing champ; Herb Darity, the New England junior welterweight champion; Larry Grandy, a Duke favorite and a Golden Gloves boxer; Tisha Luna, the first female boxer to train with Duke; Milton "Cuda" Leak, a talented welterweight; Robert Snype, a three-time Golden Gloves champion; and many more.

Although Duke could wave his magic wand over a few kids and transform them into boxing champions, it didn't happen to everybody, at least not in the ring. Many of those he touched went on to significant careers outside the roped forum, and a few even fell prey to temptation. But he treated everyone he met as if they were going to be a champion. His unselfishness

Gallucci, a lifetime friend of elite pugilist Willie Pep (*pictured*), spoke fondly of their childhood days as Hartford bootblacks.

was undeniable and never ending, which was extraordinary for someone who didn't see himself as a religious person.

Stories of Duke's gratuity could fill a book. From handing out candy to kids and filling bags of food for a needy family, to providing an elderly couple with a ride and supplying one of his boxers with a bed to lay his head on, touching another soul with kindness was never farther than his own. At no time influenced by racial prejudice, Duke detested bigotry. Since the days of Joe Louis, a real American hero and an inspiration to Duke, the talented trainer and loving father understood that boxing wanted no part of prejudice, aka "The Child of Ignorance."

Many around the fight game, such as the Duva family, learned to love and respect Duke; moreover, Lou Duva and Duke became good friends and even coached together. Boxing, as many understood, can be one big family. And, speaking of family, with so many Duke disciples still involved in the fight game, we will doubtlessly hear more forgotten tales of Giulio Gallucci for many years to come.

Chapter Seven

"EL INDIO"

GASPAR ORTEGA

Champions get up when they can't.
—Jack Dempsey

As a child, Gaspar Ortega dreamed about being a bullfighter. Picturing himself wearing a traje de luces ("suit of lights") or the traditional clothing worn into the bullring, the afternoon sun reflecting off the sequins and reflective threads of silver and gold, he could imagine the cheers as he gracefully yet systematically taunted his adversary. Although he performed in some amateur bullfights as a teenager, Ortega's dream came true in a different ring, against a more challenging adversary.

Born in Mexicali, Mexico, into a large family, Ortega learned early the art of survival—and eleven siblings can assure a near constant competitive environment. Raised in a poor Tijuana neighborhood, in a home without electricity, Gaspar always felt challenged. Needing an outlet, he turned to pugilism. A brief amateur career would reach a pinnacle when the lanky Mexican fighter captured the Golden Gloves as a flyweight in 1950. The phrase, "este niño es Bueno," quickly became as common as his victories. His next step seemed logical: Ortega turned pro in 1953.

Fighting out of San Luis Río Colorado, Mexico (the city marks the state border with Baja, California), Ortega successfully battled his way through regional competition before relocating to New York in 1954. If he was serious about the ring, which he was, there was no better place to forge a career than the "City." In less than three months, he fought three times

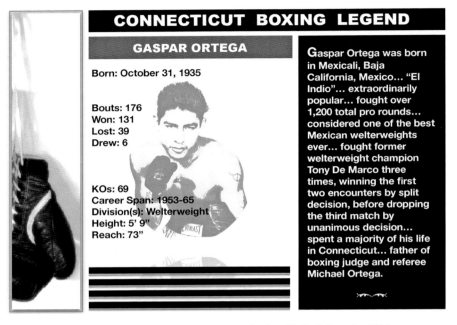

CONNECTICUT BOXING LEGEND

GASPAR ORTEGA

Born: October 31, 1935

Bouts: 176
Won: 131
Lost: 39
Drew: 6

KOs: 69
Career Span: 1953-65
Division(s): Welterweight
Height: 5' 9"
Reach: 73"

Gaspar Ortega was born in Mexicali, Baja California, Mexico... "El Indio"... extraordinarily popular... fought over 1,200 total pro rounds... considered one of the best Mexican welterweights ever... fought former welterweight champion Tony De Marco three times, winning the first two encounters by split decision, before dropping the third match by unanimous decision... spent a majority of his life in Connecticut... father of boxing judge and referee Michael Ortega.

Gaspar Ortega was inducted into the Connecticut Boxing Hall of Fame in 2006.

in Madison Square Garden (1-1-1). Impressed by what they saw, Garden management felt they had discovered a treasure. By the middle of the decade, he was packaged as "El Indio" (his mother was a Zapotec Indian). Placed beneath an ornate headdress, he was matched with competition such as "Tex" Gonzalez and Isaac Logart.

On November 23, 1956, Gaspar Ortega began a trilogy against elite fighter Tony DeMarco. And it would put him into the history books. In their first meeting, at Madison Square Garden, the lanky Mexican, a 5-1 underdog, captured a split decision over the ex-welterweight champion from Boston. DeMarco had entered the battle with an intimidating record of 51-7-1. Ortega, in contrast to most who faced the Hub fighter, successfully shut down his rival's artillery. It was no simple task. Yet, less than a month later, Ortega did it again in a rematch. To prove his point, El Indio sent DeMarco through the ropes in the opening round. In the rubber match, DeMarco, inside Boston Garden, delivered a ten-round unanimous decision against the Mexican. As opposed to his previous battles against his rival, he began with an early body assault that seemed to slow Ortega. Also, the Hub fighter was battling for his fistic life, and he knew it.

Ortega fought eight times in 1957 and posted a record of 4-4. Viewed as a contender, he even split a pair of battles against "Kid" Gavilan. Slipping a bit in 1958, Ortega composed a record of 2-3-1, with back-to-back losses against Don Jordan—the latter winning the welter title in his very next contest. In defense of "El Indio," Jordan was nearly unstoppable during this period of his career. Ortega closed out the decade by putting together a 4-4 record in 1959. A split-decision victory over Benny "Kid" Paret at Madison Square Garden kept him in the welterweight mix. But it was going to be difficult to stay there. Popular with fight fans, thanks primarily to his television exposure, Gaspar Ortega took a record of 50-17-2 into a new decade.

The 1960s marked Ortega's final term in professional boxing, but not before he added significantly to his resume. Posting a record of 7-3 in 1960, he battled Emile Griffith, a rising star in the welter ranks, to a split-decision Garden loss before punching out six consecutive victories.

Beginning the next year (1961) with battles against Carmen Basilio (L, UD 10), Benny Paret (W, UD 10) and Emile Griffith (L, TKO 12), it was clear that Ortega had little to prove. Nobody in the welter ranks was anxious to fight any of these three boxers, let alone in consecutive battles. Ortega's latter contest against Griffith was for the world welterweight title. Knocked down twice in the seventh round, Ortega fought his heart out against the future elite fighter, but Griffith proved too tough.

Always a gentleman, not to mention a sharp dresser, Gaspar Ortega was extraordinarily popular with fight fans.

From the second half of 1962 until he finally hung up the gloves in the fall of 1965, the crafty welterweight added to his totals and finished with a record of 131-39-6. From having fought a notable trilogy against Tony DeMarco and being honored with a parade in Tijuana, to splitting a pair of battles against "Kid" Gavilan and facing world-class competition such as Carmen Basilio, Nino Benvenuti, Ralph Dupas, Emile Griffith, Don Jordan and Denny Moyer, the sharp-dressed Mexican fighter left nothing on the table, as they say. Nothing. Gaspar Ortega was a ring legend. In 1968, he moved his wife and four children to Connecticut. Heavily involved with the East Haven community, he has always been beloved and respected by everyone he comes into contact with. In a testament to his skills as a father, his son Mike Ortega became a world-class boxing referee.

Notable Connecticut Battles, 1910–19

Date	Winner/Decision/Rounds	Loser	Venue/Location
April 21, 1910	Leo Houck, D 12	Dick Nelson	New Haven
February 27, 1912	Joe Jeannette, TKO 6	Andy Morris	Casino/New Haven
November 20, 1913	Packy McFarland, NWS 10	Johnny "Kid" Alberts	Auditorium/Waterbury
December 29, 1913	Jess Willard, KO 9	George Rodel	Casino/New Haven
April 23, 1914	"Lockport" Jimmy Duffy, NWS 10	Sam Robideau	Auditorium/Waterbury
April 15, 1915	Leach Cross, NWS 15	Walter Mohr	Auditorium/Waterbury
April 30, 1915	Sam Robideau, NWS 15	Walter Mohr	Casino Hall/Bridgeport
November 11, 1915	Leo Houck, D, NWS 3	Bill Fleming	Falcon Hall/Meriden
November 25, 1915 ***	Silent Martin, W, NWS 15	Al McCoy	Auditorium/Waterbury
December 17, 1917	Benny Leonard, TKO 5	Chick Brown	Arena/New Haven
April 29, 1918	Lew Tendler, W 15	Willie Jackson	Arena/New Haven
November 13, 1918	Johnny Dundee, NWS 6	Lou Bogash	State Armory/Bridgeport
May 26, 1919	Larry Williams, D, NWS, 8	Kid Norfolk	Casino Hall/Bridgeport
September 1, 1919	Joe Lynch, L, NWS, 10	Pete Herman	Driveway Park/Waterbury
September 30, 1919	Panama Joe Gans, D, NWS, 8	Eddie Tremblay	Casino Hall/Bridgeport
* Uncertain	** Fight of the Decade	*** Title Fight	

Chapter Eight

THE MAGNIFICENT

MARLON STARLING

Fame doesn't make me any different. I am the same man now who grew up in the hard streets of Panama. I am just myself. I always will be. Whoever wants to talk to me, talks to me. Whoever loves me, loves me for who I am.
—*Roberto Duran*

It has happened so many times in boxing that you often think the Thunder Gods of the ring planned it that way: the emergence of the right person at the right time. Commonly referred to as perfect timing, many believe it an act of divine intervention or maybe, just maybe, the act of an insightful individual. You know, someone who recognized opportunity when they saw it and decided to "go for it."

There are some who don't remember that both professional and amateur boxing was outlawed in 1965 by act of the Connecticut State General Assembly. The unconscionable decree immediately shelved the future of half a generation of potential ring stars from the state. Unlike in the past, teaching boxing in school was long gone from most curriculums. And we witnessed the result: bullying—using superior strength or influence to intimidate someone, typically to force him or her to do what one wants. The same parents who complained that their son or daughter was being bullied in school were the same individuals who wanted no part of boxing in an academic environment. At-risk boys and girls looking for an alternative to gangs and a haven from the social fears of the day could no longer look to

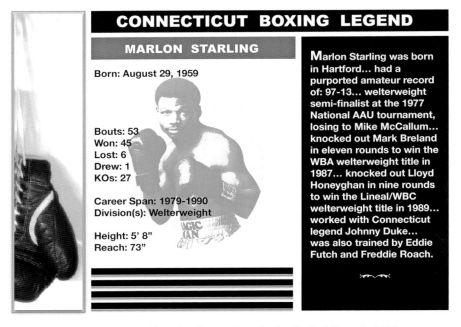

CONNECTICUT BOXING LEGEND

MARLON STARLING

Born: August 29, 1959

Bouts: 53
Won: 45
Lost: 6
Drew: 1
KOs: 27

Career Span: 1979-1990
Division(s): Welterweight

Height: 5' 8"
Reach: 73"

Marlon Starling was born in Hartford... had a purported amateur record of: 97-13... welterweight semi-finalist at the 1977 National AAU tournament, losing to Mike McCallum... knocked out Mark Breland in eleven rounds to win the WBA welterweight title in 1987... knocked out Lloyd Honeyghan in nine rounds to win the Lineal/WBC welterweight title in 1989... worked with Connecticut legend Johnny Duke... was also trained by Eddie Futch and Freddie Roach.

Marlon Starling was inducted into the Connecticut Boxing Hall of Fame in 2005.

pugilism as a cost-effective outlet. More important, the tutoring, mentoring and education and life skills that so many were taught both in and out of the ring essentially disappeared.

Enter Marlon Starling, born on August 29, 1959, in Hartford. Genetically blessed, the youngster with the million-dollar smile was the initial step of a magic recipe: Stir in a bit of Johnny Duke—on second thought, stir in a bit more. Now, to be sure, add a pinch of Manny Leibert and F. Mac Buckley and slowly blend in members of the Connecticut Boxing Guild. Add a few more secondary components and, voilà!—boxing's triumphant return to Connecticut in 1975. Naturally, it wasn't that simple. But thankfully, the ingredients were there.

MEANWHILE, UNDETERRED BY THE shortsightedness of the Connecticut State General Assembly was the Bellevue Square Boys Club. Under Johnny Duke's watchful eye, the instructor was doing everything possible to keep the Connecticut talent he saw in his crystal ball from leaving the state or even abandoning their love of the sweet science. One of the kids he was fond of and was working with was Marlon Starling. On his way to reaching the height of five feet, eight inches, the youngster had the heart and desire Duke looked for in ring talent.

On February 12, 1972, Duke transported a group of his Bellevue Square Boys Club (BSBC) boxing members to Lowell, Massachusetts, to compete in the Twenty-Fourth Annual Silver Mittens (precursor to the Golden Gloves) boxing championship being held at the National Guard Armory. Starling, age twelve, defeated Gary Hall, the 112-pound defending champion.[41] Returning to Lowell on March 10, 1972, Starling next topped Dennis Freeman, a local youngster, in the 112-pound category.

When the Twenty-Fifth Annual Silver Mittens competition in Lowell concluded in May 1973, BSBC in Hartford had five title winners and a second-place finisher: Norm Jennings (70 pounds), Steve Hillyard (80 pounds), Mike Nelson (runner-up, 90 pounds), Chris Everett (100 pounds), Marlon Starling (127 pounds) and Larry Copes (135 pounds).

Fast-forward to May 31, 1974, as Marlon Starling was named the outstanding boxer of Silver Mittens Boxing. Scoring a second-round knockout over local Tom Skerkas to win the 135-pound title, Starling turned many heads at the six-week Lowell event. Later, in August 1974, the youngster picked up the National Junior Olympic championship in the 147-pound division. His three years boxing at the Bellevue Square Boys Club, located only a stone's throw from his home, enabled "Moochie," as his friends and family called him, to pick up one of twelve prestigious titles sought by over 5,500 youngsters between the ages of twelve and fifteen. Quick to compare the adolescent to Sugar Ray Robinson, Johnny Duke saw nothing but potential in his speedy and ring-savvy student; moreover, the coach was quick to note the manners and temperament of his protégé. With his picture adorning the sports section of the August 20, 1974 issue of the *Hartford Courant*, Starling was pushed into the forefront of city boxing precisely in time for the sport's resurrection.[42]

Starling's amateur march continued, and the trophies in his Hartford bedroom soon occupied multiples tables. On May 3, 1977, five Hartford boxers, three from BSBC—Steve Hilyard (125 pounds), Tony Moore (132 pounds) and Marlon Starling (147 pounds), and two from the Parker Sands Athletic Club, Kevin Anderson (175 pounds) and heavyweight Harold Rice—found themselves in Winston-Salem, North Carolina, participating in the AAU 1977 Boxing Championships. More than 450 pugilists from all over the United Sates participated in three-round contests that eventually determined champions in all eleven divisions. "The Road to Moscow [site of the 1980 Olympics]," as it was billed, had every participant excited beyond belief. Thankfully, all five Hartford boxers made it through the third round. And Starling and Anderson became the first boxers to reach the semifinals of the National AAU Boxing Championship since 1959. Despite both unable to go any further, it was an enormous accomplishment. (Starling lost a decision to Michael McCallum of Miami, Florida.) Both fighters went on to participate on the United States AAU boxing team, which included: Israel Acosta (106 pounds), Jerome Coffee (112 pounds), Rocky Lockridge (119 pounds), Johnny Bumphus (125 pounds), Anthony Fletcher (132 pounds), Thomas Hearns (139 pounds) and Greg Page (heavyweight). By November 1977, Starling, who had been boxing since he was about eleven, began training out of the Nelson Memorial Gym in the Charter Oak Terrace section of Hartford. The facility, named after fighter Donnie Nelson, was being operated by attorney F. Mac Buckley.

Drawing to the close of his amateur career, which would finish at a purported record of 97-13, Marlon Starling, along with Marcus Starks (80-17), announced their intention of turning pro in late June 1979. Both

Marlon Starling poses next to one of the displays inside the Connecticut Boxing Hall of Fame.

A display of Marlon Starling boxing memorabilia inside the Connecticut Boxing Hall of Fame.

fighters were being trained by F. Mac Buckley and looked to matchmaker Vito Tallarita to fix them on a July 27 fight card.[43]

In his professional debut, Marlon Starling dropped Albany southpaw Tim LaValle at the 1:04 mark of the third round. The Hartford boxer went to the body early to slow his antagonist, and it worked. LaValle was not strong enough to mount a significant offense against Marlon "the Magnificent."

Chapter Nine

GREAT VENUES

Nobody owes anybody a living, but everybody is entitled to a chance.
—Jack Dempsey

Prior to the American Revolution, British troops engaged in boxing at many of the seaport towns along the coastline of the Connecticut colony. No ring was needed—or rules, for that matter—simply a challenge. After all, a person must be unshakeable in their beliefs, desires and pursuits, and they must be willing to defend their honor. There were times when that defense cost a person their life.

Rules, or guidelines, were soon developed to distinguish victory from murder. In 1838, the United States informally adopted the London Prize Ring Rules. The new rules provided for a ring twenty-four feet square bounded by two ropes. So, wherever you could find level ground, or flooring, and were able to set the stage, that was your venue. As boxing always walked the line of legality, depending on the country, state and era you happened to live in, discreet boxing forums became the norm. Early matches were frequently held in remote areas to prevent intervention by the authorities. Even floating alternatives, such as barges, were used as venues, as they could be located in waters outside U.S. legal jurisdiction.

True to the American spirit, once folks realized the entertainment factor associated with the sweet science, participation and observation came at a price. While promoting boxing could be a profitable endeavor, factors such as demographics and resources often determined success. Simply stated, location was paramount to the success of a promotion.

A plaque commemorating Morgan G. Bulkeley Stadium, located about one hundred yards off Franklin Avenue in Hartford. The facility was demolished in 1960.

Not every professional boxing match held in Connecticut was recorded, but many were. By using this information, an accurate picture of professional boxing in the state can be painted. Historically speaking, the top ten markets—based on frequency—for professional boxing in Connecticut were (in order): Hartford (including East and West), New Haven, Bridgeport, Waterbury, Stamford, New London, New Britain, Norwalk, Meriden and Milford. This does not mean that professional boxing wasn't conducted elsewhere. It was, but with far less prevalence. This data does not take into consideration casino boxing (1992–present), which will be dealt with separately.

Examining the ten markets, listed alphabetically, and their venues seems only proper.

BRIDGEPORT

It surprises some to learn that Bridgeport was a popular fight location. Truth be told, it held more contests than New London and Stamford combined.

Popular venues hosting Bridgeport boxing included Casino Hall, Hedges Stadium, Newfield Park, Park City Theater, State Armory and State Street Arena.

WHEN YOU THINK OF Bridgeport's Casino Hall, Harry Greb comes to mind. While his exciting fight against Clay Turner in 1918 may be one reason, so, too, is his battle with the "Zulu Kid" on January 29. Although scheduled for fifteen rounds, the latter bout was halted near the end of the fourteenth, because the 10:30 p.m. curfew was approaching. Yep, a curfew. Then there were the native Bridgeport boxers, and there were many, such as Lou Bogash, who made his professional debut at Casino Hall in May 1915.

Some fight fans still recall the sporadic shows held at Hedges Stadium in the 1950s. The promotions were anchored by some solid Connecticut draws, such as Willie Pep (1955), Eddie Compo (1952) and Chico Vejar (1951).

HARTFORD

As the most popular professional boxing market in the state of Connecticut, Hartford has greatly contributed to the rich history of pugilism.

Popular venues hosting Hartford boxing included Auditorium, Auditorium Outdoor Arena, Bulkeley Stadium, Capitol Park Arena, Church Street Auditorium, Civic Center (Assembly Hall), Crown Theater, Foot Guard Hall, Grand Theater, South Park Arena, State Armory, State Theater and the Velodrome, to name some.

WITH NEARLY FIFTY VENUES conducting professional boxing in the Capitol City, we will focus only on a few.

Best known as the location of Babe Ruth's final ballgame—a charity contest on September 30, 1945—Morgan G. Bulkeley Stadium, aka Wethersfield Avenue Grounds, aka Clarkin Field, was opened in 1928. The facility was located at Hanmer and George Streets, off Franklin Avenue, and had a capacity of 12,500. It was sold in 1955 and demolished. The first question out of every fight fan's mouth when you mention venues seems to be, Who fought there? Providing a few names and specifics can help frame the contribution of the venue. In a terrific upset, hometown favorite Frankie O'Brien defeated Harry Ebbets on May 22, 1919. A mere decade later, O'Brien would even adorn the cover of *The Ring* magazine.

Still the headquarters and armory of the First Company Governor's Footguard of the state of Connecticut, this building (Governor's Foot Guard Hall) is located at 159 High Street in Hartford.

In another outstanding local affair, "Battling" Battalino took a hard-fought victory over Waterbury feather Eddie Lord on June 5, 1929. In his next fight, Battalino met "Panama" Al Brown at the same venue. And, on June 13, 1940, a frustrated Jimmy Leto, having dropped his antagonist seven times in the first round, won his battle over Saverio Turiello but had to go the distance to do it.

Foot Guard (Footguard) Hall was a Romanesque Revival brick building erected in 1888 for the First Company Governor's Footguard, a ceremonial military company. Elite pugilist Tommy Ryan appears to have christened the venue for the sport on May 22, 1894, with a third-round knockout of novice Jack Flavey. Hartford pugilist Steve Ward won the last notable battle at the facility on November 1, 1960, by knocking out Jesse Watson. Taking place between these battles were over 150 boxing cards, most including six bouts or thirty-eight rounds and featuring many notable pugilists, including Louis "Kid" Kaplan, Billy Petrolle, Paul Berlenbach, Jack Delaney, Johnny Risko, Battling Battalino—you get the picture. Local talent simply thrived at the venue. The facility still stands at 159 High Street.

Velodromes, or stadiums containing a cycle-racing track with steeply banked curves, were popular during the Roaring Twenties. The Velodrome

Corporation, independent from those who handled bicycle racing, staged fistic entertainment at the Velodrome (Hurley Stadium) in Hartford. The corporation's matchmaker was George Mulligan, who was followed by Homer C. Rainault of Holyoke. Designed to hold fifteen thousand people—eleven thousand bleacher seats and four thousand reserved seats—the facility's first fistic contest was the featherweight championship of the world between Meriden's Kid Kaplan and Bobby Garcia on June 28, 1926. As Kaplan was victorious, it contributed to the perfect setting. Bat Battalino made his professional boxing debut at the venue on June 6, 1927. Jimmy Slattery's ten-round points victory over Connecticut-born Maxie Rosenbloom on August 30, 1927, for the vacant NBA world light heavyweight crown was one of the fistic highlights of the venue. Championship battles were rare, especially between two elite boxers.[44] Other notable pugilists who fought there include Mike Dundee, Harry Ebbets and Lou Brouillard. The Velodrome was sold on July 29, 1929, for $1,030 (plus warrants for back taxes), first to Thomas Santangelo, followed shortly after to the Ed Hurley Boxing Club. The facility, renamed Hurley Stadium, was quickly renovated to seat twenty-three thousand fight fans—nine thousand ringside, fourteen thousand side stands and bleachers. Located near 100 East River Drive in East Hartford, the stadium was razed in 1933.[45]

Following the battle between Terry McGovern and Young Corbett on November 28, 1901, no permits for Hartford boxing exhibitions were issued for nearly a decade.[46]

MERIDEN

Meriden has always been a fight town, or so it seems. Be it the early days of the Lenox Athletic Club or simply the career of Louis Kaplan, the city, located halfway between New Haven and Hartford, managed to attract considerable talent. Prior to Kaplan, the club featured stars such as Young Mack and Buck Deno. With the cessation of boxing bouts in Hartford and vicinity in the mid-1910s, the boxing community looked no farther than Meriden.

Popular venues hosting boxing included City Hall Auditorium, Crescent Athletic Club (AC), Falcon Hall, Hanover Park, Lenox Hall, Myer's Gymnasium, Palace Theater, Pulaski Hall, Roll-a-Way Rink, Silver City Athletic Club (AC), Silver City Stadium, State Armory and Turner Hall.

CITY HALL AUDITORIUM WELCOMED professional boxing in early 1920. And it quickly became Kid Kaplan's second home. At the venue from 1920 until 1923, the elite fighter took victories over "Battling" Green (Hartford), Joe Hall (Bridgeport), Sammy Waltz (Hartford), "Kid" Lewis (Waterbury), Billy Murphy, Pete McDonald, Billy DeFoe, Freddie Jacks, Hughie Hutchinson, Artie Rose, Johnny Lisse, Eddie Wagner, Mickey Travers (from New Haven) and Harvey Bright.[47] But Kaplan also took a rare loss in his hometown, to rival Babe Herman on December 18, 1922.

An undefeated Eddie Compo won his twenty-first professional battle at the Auditorium on February 26, 1946. And, in 1951, Val Callahan promoted the final bout at the venue, as Meriden's Jackie O'Brien defeated Mario Pacheco.

MILFORD

Entertainment, including boxing promotions, has always been driven by market factors. In 1930, Hartford had a population of 164,000, while Milford had less than 13,000. Yet, because of a venue such as Walnut Beach Stadium, Milford was able host some solid ring battles with extraordinary talent.

FROM 1927 UNTIL 1941, at Walnut Beach Stadium, fight fans could witness the pugilistic skills of artisans such as Kid Kaplan, Joe Banovic, Cocoa Kid, Jackie Davis, Nathan Mann, Tony Shucco, Bob Pastor, Johnny Bellus, Melio Bettina, Harry Jeffra and Fritzie Zivic. Also, "Battling" Siki took a four-round winning effort over Tommy Hamby in his professional debut on August 16, 1930. During an exceptionally difficult economic time, matchmaker Al Caroly did a splendid job constructing his fight cards, and he never forgot about the local pugilists.[48]

NEW BRITAIN

Among the southernmost of the communities encompassing Hartford's metropolitan region, New Britain has a history as a manufacturing center. And it's no coincidence that its greatest percentage growth in population (1900–10) paralleled its frequency in boxing promotion.

Popular venues hosting New Britain boxing included Bandeck's Hall, the Casino, Stanley Arena, Dixie Avenue AC, Hanna's Armory, Hardware City AC, Lyceum Theater, National AC, Pastime AC, Stanley Arena, T.A.B. Hall and Turner Hall.

On January 1, 1901, the legendary Joe Gans was given a controversial eleventh-round victory over Gus Gardner. Referee John Willis disqualified Gardner for repeatedly ignoring warnings not to clinch. The clash for the world lightweight title was held at the Casino in New Britain. Regardless of the abrupt verdict, to have a pugilist as talented as Gans inside your venue was a great way to begin a new year. Pugilists Tommy Sullivan (1901), Tommy Feltz (1901), George Byers (1901) and Willie Fitzgerald (1903) also did battle at the Casino.

Finally receiving his boxing permit, William W. Hanna had a brief run as a promoter in New Britain at the Armory. According to the *Hartford Courant*:

> *Mr. Hanna had placed an application before the license committee three years ago, for a boxing permit, and at a hearing given by then, Judge Cooper, the corporation counsel, said, "boxing was against the law." Mr. Hanna spoke up and said that boxing matches were held in twelve or thirteen other cities in the state. It was funny if there was one law for one city and a different law in another city. Prize fighting was against the law, but it was scientific entertainment that he proposed to stage. He did not believe in condemning a thing before giving it a fair trial.*[49]

Elite boxer Jack Britton found his way to New Britain to capture a points victory over Eddie Moran at Hanna's Armory on November 2, 1914. Returning on Christmas Day, Britton then took a points victory over Joe Hyland. Boxing at the Armory lasted until the fall of 1915.

The old Stanley Arena was located on Church Street in New Britain. Handling roughly one hundred major shows (from 1927 until 1928, from 1937 until 1949 and from 1953 until 1957), it was initially the place to be on Friday night. This was also a time of improved economic conditions in the city. In the 1920s and '30s, it attracted boxers such as Bat Battalino, Ruby Bradley, Joey Zodda (New Britain), Paul Junior and Sal Bartolo. In the 1940s, fight night at the Arena shifted from Fridays to Mondays and attracted fighters such as Billy Ivy (Hartford), Willie Pep (Hartford/Middletown),[50] Phil Terranova, Lulu Constantino, Ike Williams, Joey LaMotta, Dennis Pat

Brady (Hartford) and Carmine Fatta. Unable to attract quality fighters after this period, boxing at the Stanley declined.

New Haven

As mentioned, in 1930, Hartford had a population of 164,000. Well, New Haven wasn't far behind at over 162,000. With over thirty venues hosting professional boxing at one time or another, New Haven, a city that served as co-capital of Connecticut from 1701 until 1873, was the second-most-popular fight market in the state.

Popular venues hosting New Haven boxing included the Arena, the Casino, Music Hall, Nutmeg Stadium, Veterans Memorial Coliseum and many others.

A MAJORITY OF PROFESSIONAL boxing contests in the city were held at the New Haven Arena. The multipurpose facility, located on Grove Street in the heart of the city, serviced promoters in a variety of fields and was home to a number of professional and amateur sports teams. First opened in 1914, it burned down in 1924, reopened in 1927 and was finally closed in 1972. Although it struggled with ownership over the years, its location and capacity—it held over four thousand spectators—made it an attractive venue for many years. It was demolished in 1974, having essentially been replaced after the opening of the New Haven Coliseum.

From 1914 until 1920, a number of talented boxers found their way to the Arena: Frankie Burns, Leach Cross, Knockout Brown, Solider Barfield, Benny Leonard, Johnny Dundee, Lew Tendler and Kid Kaplan. Perhaps the most challenging battle of the decade, at least from the venue's perspective, was the bout between Harry Williams and Bunny Ford. The hometown rivals drew such passionate supporters that police stopped the clash in the fourth round for fear that that the near-capacity crowd would evolve into a riot.

During the 1920s and '30s, the Arena welcomed Bat Battalino, Joe Glick, Tony Canzoneri, James J. Braddock, "Cocoa Kid," Petey Sarron, Johnny Jadick, Ben Jeby, Lou Brouillard, Bob Olin, Nathan Mann, Maxie Rosenbloom, Melio Bettina, Lou Ambers, Frankie Klick, John Henry Lewis and Fred Apostoli.

The war years and the Fabulous Fifties attracted popular pugs such as Willie Pep, Aldo Spoldi, Allie Stolz, Chalky Wright, Tami Mauriello, Phil

Completed in 1909, this Classical Revival State Armory and Arsenal in Hartford is the largest such facility in the state and serves as headquarters of the Connecticut Military Department.

Terranova, Al "Bummy" Davis, Bobby Ruffin, Bob Montgomery, Willie Joyce, Lulu Constantino, Jimmy Carter, Tony Janiro, Beau Jack, Jock Leslie, Vic Cardell, Sandy Saddler, Joe Baksi, Paul Pender, Joey Giardello, Sugar Ray Robinson, Rocky Graziano, George Benton, "Kid" Gavilan, Chico Vejar and finally, Henry Hank. Eddie Compo knocked out Lindy Miller in his professional debut on September 11, 1944.

A few comments regarding other venues: Home to only a couple dozen events, the Casino did manage to host Joe Jeannette (1912), Johnny Coulon (1912) and Jess Willard (1913). At the turn of the nineteenth century, the Music Hall attracted heavy-hitter Casper Leon (1898) and, later, Kid Kaplan (1920). Over at Nutmeg Stadium, Frankie Genaro (1923), Young Stribling (1924), Cuddy DeMarco (1924) and Battling Battalino (1927) all laced 'em up. Sugar Ray Leonard knocked out Javier Muniz in the opening round of their battle at Veterans Memorial Coliseum on March 19, 1978.

Greatest Fights—New Haven Arena

Date	Winner/Result/Rounds	Loser	Comments
October 29, 1915	Harry Williams, NC 4	Bunny Ford	Bout stopped due to intense rivalry
October 24, 1932	Joe Banovic, PTS 10	Al Gainer	Banovic down 3X, gains unjust verdict
March 20, 1933	Tony Shucco, PTS 7	Al Gainer	Shucco floored 2X
May 15, 1933	Al Gainer, PTS 10	George Nichols	Nichols floored 3X, Gainer down once
November 9, 1933	Ben Jeby, PTS 10	Al Rossi	Jeby floored final round, yet still wins
April 23, 1034	Maxie Rosenbloom, D 10	Al Gainer	Extremely close battle
April 26, 1935	Jimmy Leto, PTS 10	Cocoa Kid	Extremely close battle
December 4, 1936	Johnny Bellus, D 6	Andy Callahan	Extremely close battle
October 28, 1938	John Henry Lewis, UD 15	Al Gainer	Close world light heavyweight title bout
December 6, 1938	Nathan Mann, TKO 7	George Fitch	Fitch down multiple times
September 16, 1940	Julie Kogon, PTS 10	Paul Junior	Kogon wins thanks to sharp counter-punching
October 7, 1946	Nathan Mann, PTS 10	John Thomas	Over 6,000 fans
October 6, 1947	Johnny Greco, TKO 3	Tommy Ciarlo	Ciarlo down 5X
September 26, 1949	Jimmy Beau, KO 3	Al Winn	A six-round semi-final
April 24, 1950	Rocky Graziano, KO 3	Danny Williams	Williams down 3X
June 12, 1950	Tommy Collins, PTS 10	Eddie Compo	Compo trounced

NC = No Contest, PTS = Points Victory, D = Draw

NEW LONDON

New London, with over a dozen venues, was the sixth-most-popular professional fight market in the state. Comparable to the Stamford market, the city hosted more battles than Meriden and Milford combined.

Popular city venues hosting boxing included the Armory, Lawrence Hall, Lyceum Theater, Ocean Beach Auditorium, the Opera House, Thames Arena and about a dozen others.

FROM 1911 UNTIL 1917, Lawrence Hall, at 15 Bank Street, conducted boxing shows. The building was owned by Joseph Lawrence, founder of Lawrence & Company, a whaling, sealing and shipping firm. Built in 1856, the exhibition hall held twelve hundred persons. When a fire destroyed the structure, a new building was constructed on the site in 1920. Of the pugilists who fought in the Hall, a few are called to mind: Johnny "Kid" Alberts, Harry Condon and Al Shubert. David Palitz, a talented hometown welterweight, made his debut at the Hall on October 10, 1912. Speaking of welters, New London's legendary Abe Hollandersky, the prolific exhibition boxer, battled out of the Hall.[51]

Over at the Opera House, in 1901, some talented pugilists went to scratch, including "Mysterious" Billy Smith, New London's own Mosey King, Tommy Feltz, Austin Rice and the incomparable George Dixon.

From about 1930 until 1933, Friday night meant boxing at the Thames Arena. The opening-night boxing card saw Bobby Mays take a points victory over the prolific Phil Richards on August 22, 1930. The cards, often five bouts, or thirty-four rounds, typically featured good, but not great, New England boxers. Among the better boxers were Jack Roper, World Colored Heavyweight Champion Obie Walker, the popular Joe Russo, "Big Boy" Burlap and "Cocoa Kid."

NORWALK

Located in southwestern Connecticut, in southern Fairfield County, on the northern shore of Long Island Sound, Norwalk lies within both the New York and Bridgeport metropolitan areas. As a matter of fact, Norwalk, with about two dozen venues, was the eighth-most-popular professional fight market in the state. The city hosted over twice as many battles as Danbury.

Popular venues hosting city boxing included the Armory, the Auditorium, Crystal Arena, Stack Arena and others.

TUESDAY NIGHTS WERE ALL about boxing at Crystal Arena. From 1946 to 1965, plenty of New England pugilists had theirs names affixed to five-bout, or thirty-four-round, fight cards at the Norwalk venue. Among the memorable names were Jimmy Carter, Ike Williams, Melio Bettina, Willie Pep, Joe Brown, Eddie Compo, Paddy DeMarco, Teddy Davis and Chico Vejar.

The most popular Crystal Arena fighters, or so it appeared for a time, were Bridgeport middleweight Joe DiMartino and New Haven middleweight Art Tatta. DiMartino, whose career spanned from 1940 to 1951, packed a punch. By 1947, the compact, five-feet, six-inch boxer held victories over George "Red" Doty, Vic Costa and Marty Servo. But a highly visible Madison Square Garden loss to Charley Fusari set him on a downward slope. DiMartino's last career victory was over elite fighter Joey Giardello on January 16, 1950. During a career that spanned a decade (1940–50), Art Tata seemed to collect victories on a monthly basis. A bit of a streaky boxer, he found himself in Madison Square Garden on October 30, 1942, a record of 19-4-3 contributing greatly to the gig. And Tata didn't disappoint, as he took a victory over Joe Governale. Happy in his role, or collecting a regular paycheck, he hung up the gloves in 1950 with a career record of 47-23-5.[52]

When fight fans recall Stack Arena, which was an excellent forum for local talent from 1939 to 1941, Lee Q. Murray's name always seems to surface. Born in St. Louis, Emanuel La Verne Murray, aka Lee Q. Murray, stood a stout six feet, three inches. Making his home in South Norwalk, the heavyweight began his professional career in 1938. Thirteen fights later, he knocked out Elza Thompson inside Madison Square Garden on June 6, 1940. Quickly establishing himself as a knockout artist, Murray had an intimidating presence by 1943. On August 9 of that year, he knocked out Harry Bobo at Oriole Park in Baltimore to capture the Maryland and Ohio Commission Heavyweight Championship. As the number-three-ranked heavyweight in the world in 1943 and 1947, Murray fought Hall of Famer Jimmy Bivens five times, winning twice.

STAMFORD

Approximately halfway between Manhattan and New Haven, or about thirty-eight miles from each, Stamford would eventually be considered part of the Greater New York metropolitan area. With a bit over a dozen venues, Stamford was the fifth-most-popular professional fight market in the state. The city hosted more battles than Meriden and Milford combined.

Popular venues hosting Stamford boxing included the Armory, Columbus Hall, Elk's Hall and Mitchell Field.

THE ARMORY HOSTED BOXING from 1923 to 1947 and attracted many regional fighters, including Eddie Mack (Stamford), Willie Angelo (Stamford), Young Mulligan (Norwalk), Pete August (Bridgeport), Steve Smith (Bridgeport), Mike Esposito (Stamford), Ted Lowry (North Haven) and Lee Q. Murray (South Norwalk). When the latter two rival fighters met on January 27, 1947, Lowry, who had hit the canvas five times, couldn't come to scratch for the fifth round.

From 1925 to 1958, Columbus Hall was the venue for over one hundred professional boxing matches. Similar to the Armory, the venue relied on local and regional talent, including Tony Travers (New Haven), Rudy Marshall (Stamford), Nick Christy (Bristol), Billy Bridges (Norwalk), Eddie Moore (Bridgeport), Willie Lewis (Stamford), Sheik Johnny Leonard (Wallingford), Jimmy O'Brien (Bridgeport), Phil Baker (Norwalk) and Harold "Snooks" Lacey (New Haven), to name only a few. On occasion, an elite fighter such as Jack Delaney, Cocoa Kid or Chico Vejar would find themselves on a card and create a bit more excitement.

Born in Stamford on May 12, 1909, Andrea Ettore Esposito, similar to his older brother Mike, seemed destined to become a boxer. So, at the age of fourteen, Andrea Esposito began his amateur career under the moniker "K.O. Morgan." Enormously successful, he followed with a professional boxing career that began in 1926. Ironically, the southpaw featherweight was more of a puncher and defensive boxer than a knockout artist. On April 15, 1930, a dismal performance against Panama Al Brown, by far the best competitor he had met to date, forced him to reevaluate his career path. Hanging up the gloves in 1946, Morgan was easily the most prolific fighter to come out of Stamford.

WATERBURY

Throughout the first half of the twentieth century, Waterbury, aka "Brass City," was the leading center in the United States for the manufacture of brassware. And it was a fight town. In reality, Waterbury, with about thirty venues, was the fourth-most-popular professional fight market in the state. Few realize that the city hosted nearly twice as many bouts as Stamford.

Popular venues hosting Waterbury boxing included the Auditorium, Brassco Park, Buckingham Hall, Lakewood Arena, Phoenix Arena, Randolph-Clowes Stadium, State Armory and many more.

PROFESSIONAL BOXING WAS CONDUCTED at Buckingham Hall from 1927 to 1959. A majority of the boxing card participants were regional pugilists: Leo Larrivee (Waterbury), Jack Kelly (Waterbury), Eddie Lord (Waterbury), Mickey Travers (New Haven), Arthur de Champlain (Wallingford), Jimmy Bell (New Haven) and Dick Turcotte (Waterbury), to select a few.

As was true with every market, certain good fighters slipped between the cracks. Eddie Dolan, aka "Irish Red," was one such fighter. In a career that spanned from 1931 until 1944, he compiled an impressive record of 89-9-3. He held victories over Harry Carlton, Paris Apice, Jimmy Lundy, Charley Burley, Tony Falco and Jimmy Leto, and Dolan also served in the U.S. Navy (1942–43). The southpaw welterweight was considered a solid and respectable opponent, merely a step from being a title contender.

Saturday night for fight fans meant a trip over to Phoenix Arena to watch some fisticuffs. From 1912 to 1933, some solid boxers battled it out, including local pugs: Johnny Shugrue (Waterbury), Dave Palitz (New

The majestic Mohegan Sun Casino is located along the banks of the Thames River in Uncasville, Connecticut.

London) and Charlie Pilkington (Meriden). But there were occasions when a bit better talent was enticed to the venue: Louis Kaplan, Frankie Jerome, Abe Goldstein, Lou Bogash, Midget Smith, Freddie Jacks, Young Tony Caponni, "KO" Sweeney, Al Gainer, Harry Carlton and Bob Olin.

State armories seemed to always host boxing and basketball. In Waterbury, the facility began hosting fights in 1922 and continued the practice until 1978. Although these exhibitions weren't conducted on a regular basis, they could attract some decent talent, including Johnny Curtin, Cuddy DeMarco, Johnny Summerhays and Duane Bobick. And some elite talent even made an appearance, including Louis "Kid" Kaplan, Babe Herman, Dave Shade, Willie Pep and Cocoa Kid. On December 10, 1926, Jack Delaney, in his first appearance since he won the world light heavyweight title from Paul Berlenbach, successfully defended it via TKO against "Jamaica Kid."

Chapter Ten

THE FIGHTERS AND THE FIGHTS

Everyone has a plan until they've been hit.
—Joe Louis

On May 24, 1861, Union forces crossed the Potomac River and occupied Arlington Heights. Prompted by Virginia's decision to secede from the Union, the troops fortified the area around the vacated mansion home of Confederate general Robert E. Lee and his family. It was during the occupation of nearby Alexandria that Colonel Elmer Ellsworth, commander of the Eleventh New York Infantry and a close friend of Abraham Lincoln, was shot dead by the owner of the Marshall House Inn. (The commander had merely removed a Confederate flag from its roof.) Later, Lincoln, the sixteenth president of the United States, eulogized his friend as "the greatest little man I ever met." Standing five feet, six inches, Ellsworth was ten inches shorter than his mentor, with whom he studied law back in Springfield, Illinois. Elmer Ephraim Ellsworth was the first conspicuous casualty and the first Union officer to die in the American Civil War (1861–65). The phrase "Remember Ellsworth" became a rallying cry and a tool for recruiting Union soldiers.

Hearing that cry, Connecticut provided arms, equipment, manpower, money, supplies and technology for the Union army, as well as for the Union navy. In Hartford, over at Conklin & Stevens at the "Bazaar," at 270 Main Street, they knew what war looked like and were prepared. They had recently received a large stock of army blankets, military shirts, military gloves and a wide assortment of woolen underclothing. With volunteers in mind, they had also received a shipment of boxing gloves, along with fencing foils, gloves and masks. As the manly art of boxing had entertained troops during the American Revolution, not to mention every conflict thereafter, it would also be an encampment staple during the "War between the States."

When General Lee accepted the inevitable and surrendered to Union general Ulysses S. Grant on April 9, 1865, at the Battle of Appomattox Court House, it essentially ended the conflict. Yet, only days later, on April 14, John Wilkes Booth, a Southern sympathizer, shot President Lincoln at Ford's Theatre in Washington, D.C. Seeing the Union drop its guard, Booth never heard the bell. Conflict, as he understood, never really ceases between rivals.

The Battle of Mystic Island, March 2, 1870

Less than five years after the tragic loss of President Lincoln, interest in another conflict was taking place. Two rival pugilists, Billy Edwards (121½ pounds) of New York and Sam Collyer (123½ pounds) of Baltimore, were meeting at Mystic Island, opposite Mystic, Connecticut, on Long Island Sound, for the lightweight boxing championship. The clandestine encounter, held at a fifty-acre spot owned by Judge Brewer, drew some twelve hundred spectators.

According to the *New York Herald*: "The ring—a single one—was pitched on the west side of the island, about one hundred yards from the beach. It was a very level spot, and all injurious substances, such as bits of twigs and stones, were cleared from it, while two enthusiastic individuals drove stakes."[53]

For forty rounds, the pair traded blows while inducing damage, primarily to the face of their antagonist; a round concluded when a pugilist hit the ground. As the sessions played out, each boxer—blood flowing freely from gashes and facial features—did his best to protect what little remained intact above his shoulders. A simple glance at Collyer's disfigured left cheek told the story by the thirtieth round.

The *New York Herald* saw the final round in this manner: "When Collyer received the last blow (a terrific left-hander to the jaw) he fell senseless to the ground and was carried to his corner. Time was called, but poor Sam was unconscious, and the sponge was thrown up by the second in token of defeat."[54]

As an illegal activity, prizefighting, a popular yet surreptitious diversion, was always weighed against the mighty dollar. Fueled by gamblers attracted to the odds—or the risk/reward ratio, if you will—prizefighting, as they saw it, was the perfect vehicle. Consider the following example: an investment with a risk/reward ratio of 1:9 suggests that an investor is willing to risk $1.00 for the prospect of earning $9.00. That may not sound significant today, but it was in 1870, when a worker manufacturing hardware was pocketing $2.41 a day, or $12.05 per week.

Prior to 1900

From Bridgeport, Danielson, Hartford, New Haven and New London to Naugatuck, Putnam, Waterbury, West Haven and Willimantic, boxing, often masked as exhibitions, was conducted and enjoyed. And big purses from big backers brought some of the finest pugilists in the fight game.

Prior to 1900, elite fighters such as George Dixon, Terry McGovern, Tommy Ryan and Joe Walcott fought in Connecticut.

The first Black man to win a world boxing title, George Dixon, fought Frank Maguire to a draw, over ten rounds, in Putnam on March 1, 1889. Of his fights in the state, this was perhaps the most memorable. Considered to be one of the finest small boxers ever, Dixon outgrew the bantamweight division by 1892 and began competing solely as a featherweight.

Terry McGovern, a hard-hitting Brooklyn fighter who captured both the bantamweight and featherweight titles, fought two memorable battles. He knocked out Fred Mayo in the sixth round of their April 15, 1898 fight in Waterbury, and he knocked out Eddie Sprague in the second round of their clash at the Coliseum in Hartford.

Born Joseph Youngs, Tommy Ryan scored knockouts in seventeen of his first eighteen recorded bouts. Ryan, whose ten-year hold on the middleweight crown was unrivaled, had numerous memorable Connecticut clashes, including a second-round knockout of Harry Jamieson in Waterbury on November 2, 1893; a third-round TKO of Morris Lane at Savin Rock in West Haven on April 10, 1894; and an eighth-round knockout of Jack Falvey at Foot Guard Hall in Hartford on May 22, 1894.

"Barbados" Joe Walcott, considered the greatest of the welterweights, was a tenacious warrior who took on all comers, from welterweight to heavyweight. Walcott was short yet compact, and his most memorable Connecticut skirmish was a twenty-five-round marathon draw against

"Mysterious" Billy Smith at the Park City Theater in Bridgeport on April 14, 1898. In the opinion of the *Hartford Courant*, "For the first ten rounds the sparring was probably the most clever ever witnessed in Bridgeport."[55]

Canadian-born George Byers, who won the World Colored Middleweight Championship in 1897 and may have held the World Colored Heavyweight Championship from September 14, 1898, to March 16, 1901, was one of the finest pugilists of the era. He was compact, muscular and skillful, and his rivalry with Dan Murphy was never more evident than their battle on November 11, 1897. Many believed it was one of the finest boxing matches ever held in Waterbury.

Notable Connecticut Battles, Prior to 1900

Date	Winner/Decision/Rounds	Loser	Venue/Location
May 17, 1881 **	Charles Hadley, KO 18	Professor Anderson	Bridgeport
January 19, 1888	George LaBlanche, W 3	Mike Burns	City Hall/Waterbury
February 24, 1895 *	Peter Maher, KO 2	Jack O'Rourke	Willimantic
February 28, 1895 *	Peter Maher, KO 4	Harry Jamieson	Auditorium/Hartford
January 15, 1896	Billy Smith, TKO 1	Pat Kehoe	Auditorium/Hartford
December 29, 1896	Patsey Haley, D 3	Johnny Reagan	Danielson
April 5, 1897	George Byers, D 10	Dan Murphy	Auditorium/Hartford
May 25, 1897	George Byers, D 15	Dan Murphy	Nutmeg AC/Hartford
May 31, 1897	Casper Leon, W 15	Lew Myers	Charter Oak Park/Hartford
July 2, 1897	Bobby Dobbs, W 8	James "Rube" Ferns	Hartford
September 23, 1897	Charles Goff, D 12	George Byers	Gladiator AC/Hartford
November 11, 1897 **	George Byers, D 20	Dan Murphy	Jacques Auditorium/Waterbury
February 2, 1899	Jack Bonner, TKO 10	Dick O'Brien	Coliseum/Hartford
February 22, 1899	Oscar Gardner, D 20	Martin Flaherty	Coliseum/Hartford
March 6, 1899	Austin Rice, D 20	Tim Callahan	Opera House/New London
November 9, 1899	Austin Rice, W 15	"Brooklyn" Tommy Sullivan	Auditorium/Waterbury
* Uncertain date	** Fight of the Decade		

1900–1909

Not every professional boxing match in Connecticut found its way into an official record. Of the estimated two hundred recorded battles, about half were conducted at athletic clubs. In Hartford, that would be venues such as the Empire AC and Nutmeg AC. And if a larger venue was needed, such as the Coliseum, then it would be conducted under its auspices.

Having settled and fought primarily out of Boston, Joe Walcott's proficiency as a fighter would force him to look farther outside of New England to find opponents, but not before delivering Connecticut fight fans four noteworthy battles. On September 24, 1900, he took a disqualification victory over a frustrated "Mysterious" Billy Smith at the Coliseum in Hartford. At that same venue, on December 13, 1900, Walcott knocked out "Wild Bill" Hanrahan in the twelfth round. At the Empire Athletic Club in Hartford on January 17, 1901, he was disqualified in an intense clash against "Kid" Carter. And on March 21, 1901, at the Auditorium in Waterbury, Walcott picked up a TKO over a determined Charlie McKeever.

Emerging from Waterford, a suburb of New London, was an impressive bantamweight by the name of Austin Rice. A local legend by 1903, Rice impressed with six performances. He fought Tommy Sullivan to a draw in Waterbury in December 1900. On January 18, 1901, Rice took a fifteen-round points victory over a determined Hughey Murphy in New London. Also, in New London on February 26, 1901, he grabbed an eleven-round points victory over "Brooklyn" Tommy Sullivan. In New Britain, on June 10, 1901, Rice fought Tommy Feltz to a twenty-round points victory at the Casino. At the Opera House in New London, he took a twenty-round points victory over the legendary George Dixon. And on April 17, 1902, at Poli's Theater in Waterbury, Rice drew Boston's Dave Sullivan over twenty rounds. Ironically, it was an impressive performance in a losing effort on January 14, 1903, against featherweight champion Young Corbett II that solidified Rice's position as a world-class competitor. That bout was held in Hot Springs, Arkansas.

THE FIGHT

The *Boston Post* reported on November 29, 1901, the impossible: "M'GOVERN WHIPPED, Corbett Did the Trick Early in Second Round, TERRY LOST HIS HEAD." The front-page news rang out all across America.

Jack Johnson was one of the elite fighters who found his way to Bond's Dock training camp on the Housatonic River at Stratford. It was run by mustachioed former schooner captain John C. Bond. *Library of Congress, LC-DIG-ggbain-08094 (digital file from original negative).*

The report continued:

> *Knocked out in the second round, of which one minute and 44 seconds had elapsed, was the referee's verdict of the fistic battle between "Young" Corbett of Denver, Col., and "Terry" McGovern of Brooklyn, who has held the featherweight championship unflinchingly, since he won it from George Dixon 18 months ago. Outwitted and outpointed by a fighter just as game as himself, McGovern had to lower his colors this afternoon [November 18, 1901] at the Nutmeg AC to Young Corbett within seven minutes from the start of the fight. Five thousand enthusiasts witnessed Terry's Waterloo.*[56]

In perhaps the first example of psychological ring warfare, known today as "trash talk," Corbett banged on the champion's dressing-room door before the fight and jeered him by reciting some nasty remarks about his family. Enraged prior to entering the ring, McGovern cast science to the wind. He lost before he ever entered between the ropes.

Speaking of McGovern, Bond's Dock training camp on the Housatonic River at Stratford, run by mustachioed former schooner captain John C. Bond, was located at the original landing site of the Puritan settlers of Stratford. Later, it became a popular boxing camp for fighters like John L. Sullivan, Jack Johnson and Terry McGovern.

HEAVYWEIGHT TOM SHARKEY KNOCKED out Jim McCormick in the opening round of his March 15, 1900 battle at the Coliseum in Hartford. As his only official ring appearance in the state, it was quick yet impressive.[57]

Speaking of impressive, New York welterweight Willie Lewis clashed with Mosey King at the National Athletic Club in New Britain on September 25, 1902. They had met previously in New London. Lewis dropped his antagonist—the future head boxing coach at Yale—once in the eleventh round and four times in the nineteenth round on his way to a twenty-round points victory.

On March 15, 1900, Tom Sharkey made a rare—and brief—appearance at the Coliseum in Hartford. *Library of Congress, LC-DIG-ggbain-04810 (digital file from original negative).*

Notable Connecticut Battles, 1900–09

Date	Winner/Decision/Rounds	Loser	Venue/Location
June 7, 1900	Wilmington Jack Daly, W 25	Kid McPartland	Union AC/ Waterbury
July 12, 1901*	Ned "Kid" Broad, W 15	Billy Gardner	Park City Theater/Bridgeport
February 13, 1902	Gerge Dixon, W 20	Chick Taylor	National AC/New Britain
April 7, 1902	George McFadden, KO 5	Curly Supples	Casino/New Britain
November 27, 1902	George McFadden, W 20	Patsy Sweeney	National AC/New Britain
March 9, 1903	Tommy Feltz, D 20	Austin Rice	New Britain
September 5, 1907	Jim Barry, W 6	Jack Blackburn	Savoy AC/Bridgeport
September 12, 1907	Jack Johnson, NWS 6	Sailor Burke	Smith's Theater/Bridgeport
April 26, 1909	Owen Moran, NWS 12	Frankie Neil	Anchor AC/New Haven
November 29, 1909	Mike Twin Sullivan, NWS D 12	Jimmy Gardner	Grand Opera House/New Haven
* Uncertain	NWS = Newspaper Decision		AC = Athletic Club

The "Old Master," Joe Gans simply overwhelmed Gus Gardner over eleven rounds on January 1, 1903. The New Britain fight, held at the Casino, was billed as a world lightweight championship. Unfortunately, referee John Willis had little choice but to disqualify Gardner in the eleventh round.[58]

Furious over how boxing was being conducted, the state enacted new legislation in 1903. It wasn't a surprise; cities such as Hartford had essentially stopped issuing boxing permits following the McGovern/ Corbett contest.

1910–19

Political tensions over the rise of the German empire were the principal cause of World War I (1914–18). The United States, doing its best to avoid a war in which the fighting took place on land in Europe and was generally characterized by long periods of bloody stalemate, had no choice but to enter the fray in its latter stages. Despite the conflict, not to mention the Frawley Law—limiting bouts to ten rounds and prohibiting decisions—passed by the New York legislature in 1911, boxing thrived in many cities of nearby Connecticut.[59] The frequency of professional fights held in the state more than doubled from previous years while producing the century's third most successful decade for the sport.

Barney Lebrowitz, better known as "Battling Levinsky," was the world's light heavyweight champion from 1916 to 1920. Born in Philadelphia to Jewish immigrant parents from Russia, his career, which began in 1910, would span two decades. Honestly speaking, Levinsky's appearances in Connecticut prior to 1915 were not impressive. That would change on May 27, 1918, when the pugilist tangled with Bartley Madden at the Casino in Bridgeport. Clashing over fifteen rounds, the pair went toe to toe in a slugfest that most saw in favor of Levinsky; Madden had been substituted for Eugene Brosseau. According to the *Bridgeport Telegram*: "For heavyweights the men put up a fast battle and strange though it may seem the big battler [Levinsky] waded in and fought like a slugger. He hit Madden from all angles and hammered the New Yorker....Madden, however, did succeed in rapping Levinsky four fairly hard ones and on one occasion that being the last and fifteenth round he uncorked a right to the head which staggered Levinsky."[60]

Joe Shugrue worked in vaudeville and later opened up a tavern and gymnasium in Waterbury in 1920. But to many, Shugrue, aka "Young" Shugrue, aka "Jersey Bobcat," was nothing short of an exciting pugilist. In a ring career that spanned only five years, he managed to entertain Connecticut fight fans like few others. Of his numerous appearances, a few stand out. On April 25, 1912, he took a fifteen-round points victory over Young Dyson at the Auditorium in Waterbury. At the same venue, on November 28, 1912, Shugrue took a competitive fifteen-round victory over "Philadelphia" Pal Moore. And in a losing effort, the Jersey-born pugilist put on a magnificent display against Matty Baldwin on July 3, 1913, at the Clinton AC in New Haven. Baldwin, a veteran who took twelve of the fifteen rounds, was impressed by the aggressiveness and durability of his antagonist.[61]

The first world champion—having won the featherweight title on September 4, 1916—to hail from Cleveland, Johnny Kilbane scored a tenth-round knockout over Johnny Drummie at the Auditorium in Waterbury on January 18, 1917. Returning to Connecticut on March

A pioneer of the one-two punch, Willie Lewis was a prolific and talented welterweight who hailed from New York City. *Library of Congress, LC-DIG-ggbain-08232 (digital file from original negative).*

26, 1917, he fought a controlled twelve-round draw against veteran Eddie Wallace at Park Theatre in Bridgeport. Perhaps the *Bridgeport Times and Evening Farmer* stated it best: "The champion is very quick in his movements, a marvel at infighting and always packs a dangerous punch. Like most champions he is overcautious in the ring because he wished to take no chance of losing his title."[62]

On his way to a remarkable career, Harry Greb would make three memorable stops in Connecticut during his first year as a professional fighter; incidentally, he would finish with just under 300 total career bouts (262-17-18-1). As previously mentioned, on January 29, 1918, Greb gave an outstanding performance to grab a fourteen-round newspaper verdict over "Zulu Kid." (The fight was halted due to an ordinance requiring performances to end by 10:30 p.m.) Later, on May 15, Greb captured a thrilling fifteen-round newspaper decision over "Indian" Clay Turner; specifically, Greb won eleven rounds, Turner two and two were even. Turner, who was four inches taller than Greb, managed to stagger his opponent in both the seventh and eighth rounds.[63] And, on June 24, 1918,

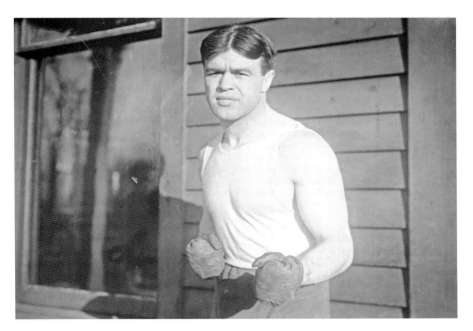

Matty (Matthew) "Bunker Hill Bearcat" Baldwin, a prolific Hub lightweight, fought in New Britain, Waterbury and New Haven. *Library of Congress, LC-DIG-ggbain-10118 (digital file from original negative).*

the "Pittsburgh Windmill" delivered, almost at will, fifteen rounds' worth of damage to Frank Carbone to capture a newspaper decision. All three battles occurred at Casino Hall in Bridgeport.

In New London, a young welterweight by the name of Dave Palitz was making a name for himself. During this decade, he would post Connecticut (points and newspaper) victories over New London's Abe Hollandersky, New Haven's Bunny Ford and Massachusetts pugilist Dave Powers. His ring career would draw to a conclusion in 1922, but not before he entered the ring against Jack Britton and competed for the Connecticut Welterweight Championship against Lou Bogash.[64]

Other appearances worth noting are the following: Dixie Kid fought (Frank Mantell) in Waterbury, Philadelphia Pal Moore clashed (Young Dyson) in New Haven, Young Otto battled (Dodo Maher) in Norwalk, and Johnny Dundee skirmished (Willie Jackson) in New Haven.

1920–29

From Prohibition, flappers and the Harlem Renaissance to the Teapot Dome Scandal, the Tulsa Race Massacre and the Scopes Trial, the Roaring Twenties was primarily an era of consumerism, creativity and outrage. Professional boxing in Connecticut nearly doubled in frequency while producing the century's second-most-successful decade for the sport. Igniting this sensational era of boxing was the Walker Law, passed in 1920. Reestablishing legal boxing in New York following the three-year ban created by the repeal of the Frawley Law, it led the way for other states to follow. The law instituted rules that better ensured the safety of combatants while polishing the image of the sport. Limiting matches to fifteen rounds, requiring the attendance of a physician, restricting certain aggressive acts such as head-butting and creating the regulatory body NYSAC (New York State Athletic Commission) sparked interest and participation. In October 1921, Connecticut followed suit.

A young teenager boxing out of the Lenox Athletic Club in Meriden found himself in the perfect place at the perfect time. Ukrainian-born Louis Kaplan possessed natural skills but needed instruction. Finding a mentor, not to mention a sparring partner, in featherweight Charlie Pilkington, a former New York State champion, was like discovering a winning lottery ticket. Engaging in over fifty bouts in his first four years in the paid ranks, Kaplan crafted his skills along a bumpy career path until spring 1921. From that point forward, he appeared unstoppable.

Of Kaplan's notable Connecticut fights in that era, a couple are worth repeating. On September 14, 1922, he took the aforementioned twelve-round points victory over Waterbury boxer Johnny Shugrue at Hanover Park in Meriden. At City Hall Auditorium in Meriden on December 18, 1922, Kaplan, who performed well over twelve rounds, took a heartbreaking loss to Babe Herman. Flooring Herman to a four-count in the opening round of their rematch, Kaplan turned the tables on March 8, 1923, at the State Armory in Meriden. When Kaplan defeated Herman in a featherweight title bout on December 18, 1925, at Madison Square Garden, the superb rivalry came to a conclusion. However, many fight fans believe that Kaplan's performance in a draw with Herman at Brassco Park in Waterbury on August 27, 1925, may have been his finest. For seven rounds, he used his right arm to block punches because of a broken finger on his right hand. Kaplan's engaging ring performances were so common that fight fans expected every Connecticut battle to be thoroughly as engrossing. As a matter of fact, for a generation, all subsequent ring performances were juxtaposed with those of Kaplan.[65]

Lou Bogash, along with his brother Patsy, grew up on Garfield Avenue in the North End of Bridgeport. Fighting out of the Acorn Club on Kossuth Street on the East Side and the Venice AC off Main Street, both Italian-born brothers were quick to impress.[66] While Patsy's professional career didn't make it to 1924, Lou's lasted until 1931. And my, what a record Lou Bogash assembled. Some, including Bill Lee, sports editor for the *Hartford Courant*, even believed he may have been Connecticut's greatest fighter to never win a championship.[67] Recalled often for having fought valiantly in unsuccessful efforts against two world champions—Jack Britton (D 12) and Jack Delaney (L 15)—Bogash held victories over "Battling" Kunz (Connecticut Light Title), Patsy Cline, Walter Mohr, Dave Palitz, Solider Bartfield, Mickey Walker, Tommy Loughran and Lou Scozza.

Jack Delaney turned pro in 1919, and manager Al Jennings took him as far as he could by 1922, before Pete "The Fox" Reilly took over and drove the fighter to a world light heavyweight title. Delaney held victories over Jackie Clark, Tommy Loughran, Paul Berlenbach, Frank Moody, Tiger

Featherweight champion Johnny Kilbane visited Connecticut twice in 1917, battling in Waterbury and Bridgeport. *Library of Congress, LC-DIG-ggbain-10280 (digital file from original negative).*

Flowers, Maxie Rosenbloom and Jack Renault, but his career faded once he turned to the heavyweight division.

Frankie O'Brien, a southpaw middleweight from Hartford, made his debut on October 18, 1923. The four-round decision at Charter Oak Park wasn't spectacular, but it was a start. After losing half of his first four battles, he posted five consecutive victories. On June 11, 1928, O'Brien found himself at the Velodrome in Hartford fighting for the New England Middleweight Title. Following a fourth-round disqualification of his opponent, Al Mello, O'Brien had his first crown. It was the confidence he needed, as he won his next fourteen fights against the likes of Frank Konchina, Jack Britton, Harry Ebbets and George Manolian. Perhaps his best fight was in a ten-round losing effort to "Gorilla" Jones in Milwaukee. It was in the semifinal

Notable Connecticut Battles, 1920–29

Date	Winner/Decision/Rounds	Loser	Venue/Location
August 21, 1920	Abe Goldstein, W, NWS 12	Young Montreal	Wethersfield Baseball Grounds/Hartford
March 29, 1921	Johnny Shugrue, PTS 15	Charlie Pilkington	Arena/New Haven
September 16, 1921	Mike Morley, PTS 12	Phil Bloom	Church Street Auditorium/ Hartford
June 16, 1924	Harry Greb, KO 6	Frank Moody	Brassco Park/Waterbury
June 23, 1924	George Manolian, D 10	Sheik Johnny Leonard	Nutmeg Stadium/New Haven
March 4, 1926	Paul Doyle, W 12	Jack Oakes	Foot Guard Hall/Hartford
September 10, 1926	Johnny Risko, D 12	Pat McCarthy	Foot Guard Hall/Hartford
August 30, 1927 ***	Jimmy Slattery, PTS 10	Maxie Rosenbloom	Velodrome/Hartford
October 22, 1927 ***	Pinky Silverberg, DQ 7	Ruby Bradley	State Armory/Bridgeport
May 22, 1929	Frankie O'Brien	Harry Ebbets	Bulkeley Stadium/Hartford
July 26, 1929	Bat Battalino, PTS 10	Panama Al Brown	Bulkeley Stadium/Hartford
September 23, 1929	Bat Battalino, PTS 15	Andre Routis	Hurley Stadium/East Hartford
*** - Title Fight			

round of the NBA middleweight title elimination series held on November 19, 1931. The fighters went at each other hammer and tongs. Hanging up the gloves in 1934, O'Brien had compiled a record of 53-12-0.

Connecticut seemed to draw more than its fair share of talent during the era. "Battling" Levinsky went ten rounds with Clay Turner in Hartford on March 16, 1920. In a less-than-satisfactory performance, but nevertheless an appearance, Harry Wills easily defeated Ray Bennett in Bridgeport n June 1, 1920. Benny Leonard outclassed Frankie Britt by taking a fifth-round TKO in Hartford on October 4, 1920. Pancho Villa impressed with a twelve-round points victory over Willie Darcy in Waterbury on March 24, 1923. And Frankie Genaro overwhelmed Frankie Daly in an easy twelve-round points victory in New Haven on July 27, 1923. Also appearing in a Connecticut ring were "Memphis" Pal Moore, Young Stribling, Billy Petrolle, Jack Sharkey and Paul Berlenbach.

1930–39

As a decade defined by the Great Depression and the advent of another world war, it surprises some to learn that professional boxing in Connecticut suffered far less than expected; incidentally, it decreased in frequency by about 15 percent. It is a figure hard to believe, based on the economic conditions. As might be expected, many elements around the fight game faced challenges. From 1932 to 1937, staying employed in the sweet science was a more difficult task than finding your next meal.[68]

Unrelenting in doling out punishment, Louis "Kid" Kaplan, who would lose only five battles before ending his career in 1933, delivered many impressive Connecticut performances. On March 18, 1930, he captured a ten-round points victory over Johnny Farr at the Arena in New Haven. In an outstanding performance, Kaplan took a ten-round victory over Connecticut's own "Battling" Battalino at Hurley Stadium in East Hartford on September 24, 1930. And at Capital Park Stadium in Hartford on September 8, 1931, he picked up a ten-round points victory over Jackie Pilkington in a bout for the New England Lightweight Championship. However, since giving up the featherweight throne, perhaps his greatest performance was his ten-round points victory over Sammy Mandell at Hurley Stadium in East Hartford on August 24, 1931. From his trademark crouched position, Kaplan discharged volley after volley of often unanswered left and right hooks to the ribs of Mandell while capturing every round.

By 1933, it felt like all the Connecticut excitement created by the career of Kid Kaplan had been passed to Bat Battalino. Granted, Kaplan handed the youngster the aforementioned decisive (decision) loss at Hurley Stadium, but it was inevitable. This was a decade that would define Battalino. He defended the world featherweight title by knocking out Ignacio Fernandez in the fifth round of a contest held at Hurley Stadium in East Hartford on July 15, 1930. Taking a fifteen-round unanimous decision over Kid Chocolate at Madison Square Garden on December 12, 1930, he seized the NYSAC world feather title. And he decisively defeated Fidel LaBarba in a "show me don't tell me" defense at Madison Square Garden on May 22, 1931. Was Battalino a streaky fighter? Yes, without question, beginning in 1930. But, was he a "cheese champion"? Not a chance.

Nelson Allen Gainer was born in Gretna, Florida, on September 6, 1906. Relocating to New Haven, he began a professional boxing career in 1930. And by 1934, Al Gainer, by which he was known, was being ranked among the contenders for the light heavyweight title. Although he would log some impressive victories over boxers like Bob Olin (1931), James J. Braddock (1931) and George Nichols (1934), it was his clash against Lou Brouillard at the Arena in New Haven that pushed him into the spotlight. Brouillard, a 2-1 favorite entering the contest, took the worst beating and loss of his career; moreover, he won only one round. Gainer's outstanding left and punishing right cross utterly battered the countenance of his antagonist until it swelled like an overblown inner tube.[69] Before the decade closed, Gainer also posted stunning victories over Al McCoy (1934), Dave Shade (1935), Tony Galento (1936), Steve Dudas (1936) and Don "Red" Barry (1937).[70]

Another career showing promise was that of Herbert Lewis Hardwick, aka Lou Hardwick, aka "Cocoa Kid," fighting out of New Haven.[71] Raised by a maternal aunt, Herbert began boxing in Atlanta at the age of fourteen. In 1932, Connecticut state senator Harry Durant spotted him in West Palm Beach, believed in his potential and sponsored his move to New Haven. Campaigning as "Cocoa Kid," he captured victories over Pancho Villa (1933), Louis Kaplan (1933), Johnny Jadick (1933) and Steve Halaiko (1934), interspersed between impressive losses to Wesley Ramey (1933) and Lou Ambers (1933). This brought him to Bat Battalino on October 23, 1934. Although Battalino beat him like a morning omelet, the Kid was unrelenting and displayed solid skills during the early rounds. Unhappy with his management, Cocoa Kid looked first to Massachusetts before heading south to New Orleans. Prolific, and ranked among the contenders in three divisions (lightweight, welterweight and middleweight), Cocoa

Kid has often been recalled for his rivalry with Holman Williams, whom he faced thirteen times.

Born in Saint-Eugene, Quebec, Canada, Lucien Pierre Brouillard, better known as Lou Brouillard, turned pro in 1928. Compiling an impressive record of 61-7, he was given a shot at the world welterweight title on October 23, 1931, at Boston Garden. Dropping rival "Young" Jack Thompson to the canvas four times, Brouillard, a resident of Danielson, was given the fifteen-round unanimous decision along with the title. Among his captivating victories during this period are Johnny Indrisano (1932), Jimmy McLarnin (1932), Mickey Walker (1933), Ben Jeby (1933), Bob Olin (1934), Al Gainer (1934) and Young Corbet III.

By 1933, Stephen Surowiecki, aka Steve Carr, was fighting out of the Arena in New Haven, and folks were beginning to notice. Having begun his professional career in the great fight market of Holyoke, Massachusetts, he would eventually find solace in Meriden. Standing five feet, ten inches tall and a light heavyweight, Carr was rugged, resilient and tireless. His 1934 trilogy against Joe Kaminski of Nanticoke, Pennsylvania, was one of the finest fought at the Valley Arena in Holyoke. The first and last were ten-round draws, while Carr took the second battle by unanimous decision. Carr's action-packed 1935 bouts against Tiger Warrington (June 24, South Park Arena) and Nathan Mann (August 29, White City Stadium) are still recalled. Holding victories over Johnny Rossi, Max Marek and Danny Hassett, he finally hung up the gloves in 1939.[72]

In 1934, another force was being nurtured in New Haven, a heavyweight by the name of Natale Menchetti, aka Nathan Mann. The five-feet, ten-inch fighter had an impressive reach of seventy-five inches and plenty of power behind his punches. His first six professional fights were knockout victories. Minus some problems getting by Rhode Island heavy Eddie Coderre, Mann sliced through his opponents like a hot knife through butter. By June 1935, he was on a Yankee Stadium undercard against Al Zappala. Mann knocked out his antagonist in the third round. His aforementioned encounter with Steve Carr was a hard-fought loss, but he would continue his winning ways thereafter. Mann's breakout year came in 1937, as four impressive victories (Abe Feldman, Arturo Godoy, Bob Pastor and Tiger Roy Williams) brought him a heavyweight title fight against the incomparable Joe Louis on February 23, 1938. In his second title defense, Louis floored Mann four times on the way to a third-round knockout victory. Mann finished the year at 4-2-1. Posting a record of 10-1 in 1940, Mann took victories over Steve Dudas and George Fitch; his only loss was to Buddy Baer. With a career record of 73-12-4, Mann had planted himself firmly in heavyweight boxing history.

John F. Monacchio, aka Johnny Mack, was a talented and powerful-punching New Britain lightweight who turned pro in 1928. After losing his first three contests, he quit boxing. Resurrecting his career in 1936, Mack posted fifteen consecutive victories before losing a battle to veteran George Daly in Great Britain. Returning to Connecticut, Mack became a streaky fighter while taking victories over Joey Costa, Joey Zodda, Howard Scott and Jimmy Vaughn. As a popular restaurateur, Mack was extremely active in Connecticut boxing; he often led delegations of dedicated Willie Pep fans to venues all across the country.

Also participating in notable ring appearances were Jack Britton, Tony Canzoneri, Midget Wolgast, Frankie Genaro, Obie Walker, Jack Delaney, Melio Bettina, Lou Ambers, Eddie Booker and many others.

1940–49

Despite World War II, this decade would be the most prolific in the history of professional boxing in Connecticut. In 1946, the first full year after the war, more professional fights were recorded in Connecticut than in any year during the twentieth century. And if you had to pick a fighter to represent the decade, if not a face to attach permanently to professional boxing in Connecticut, it would be Guglielmo Papaleo, aka Willie Pep.

A magnificent ring craftsman, Willie Pep was to the sport of boxing what Rudolf Nureyev was to ballet—the premier choreographer. Evasive, expeditious and astute, he could make a great boxer appear mediocre and a good pugilist look foolish. Turning professional in 1940, Pep was the featherweight champion of the world by 1942.

Prior to the Japanese attack on the U.S. fleet at Pearl Harbor, four fighters were making their mark on Connecticut boxing: Johnny Bellus, Eddie Dolan, Julie Kogon and Joe Polowitzer.

Turning pro in 1931, John Belous, aka Johnny Bellus, stood five feet, seven inches tall and battled out of New Haven. An exciting yet streaky lightweight, by the summer of 1937, he held victories over Jackie Davis, Charlie Baxter, Lew Feldman, Joey Costa and Phil Baker. On August 12, Bellus took an impressive eight-round points victory over Feldman in his first appearance at Madison Square Garden. Hanging up the gloves in 1944, Bellus left behind a career mark of 69-26-8, not to mention some great memories.

Eddie Dolan, aka "Irish Red" Dolan, was a talented southpaw out of Waterbury. A gifted athlete, the youngster was using his lightweight/welterweight talents to pay the bills; pugilism more of a once-a-month avocation than a job. Having begun his career in late 1931, just like Bellus, Dolan started to believe he had some talent by 1934 and proved it with victories over Harry Carlton, Paris Apice and Jimmy Lundy. By 1938, he was in the ring with veteran Midget Wolgast, and by 1939, he was battering Milo Theodorescu at Yankee Stadium on the undercard of the Henry Armstrong / Lou Ambers championship fight. Posting a career record of 89-9-3, he, like others, served his country proudly in the U.S. Armed Forces.

Fighting out of his hometown of New Haven, Julius Kogon, aka Julie Kogon, compiled an amateur record of 85-2 before turning pro in 1937. Often compared to Jewish lightweight champion Benny Leonard—the pair shared a religion and a boxing style—Kogon developed a devoted following who loved the excitement he brought to the ring. Battling until 1950, he took victories over Jimmy Vaughn, Paul Junior, Petey Scalzo and Pete Scanlon. Equally impressive, as was often the case with scrappers like Kogon, were his defeats—to Leo Rodak, Bob Montgomery, Willie Pep and Ike Williams.

If you hailed from East Hartford during the war years, nobody had to tell you that the Polowitzer brothers—Joe, Fred, Bobby and Henry—could box. Boy, could they. Joe, who began his career in 1940, was a streaky southpaw lightweight who created a stir when he split a pair of West Haven scraps against a young Beau Jack.[73]

During the war years, some outstanding fighters found themselves battling in Connecticut, including Lou Ambers, Al "Bummy" Davis, Izzy Jannazzo, Jake LaMotta, Tami Mauriello, Sandy Saddler, Marty Servo, Ike Williams and Chalky Wright,

And let's not forget about some solid Connecticut fighters who may have slipped between the cracks: light Dennis Pat Brady (Hartford), light Johnny Compo (New Haven), middle Joe DiMartino (Bridgeport), light George Dunn (Hartford), heavy Charley Eagle (Waterbury), heavy George Fitch (New Haven), feather Bobby Ivy (Hartford), light Joey Izzo (Hartford), feather Harold "Snooks" Lacey (New Haven), feather Al Moffatt (Bridgeport,) welter Angelo Radano (Norwalk), feather Eddie Reed (Hartford) and heavy Bernie Reynolds (Fairfield), to name just a few.

After the war, professional boxing flourished in Connecticut and attracted some popular names, including Joe Brown, Jimmy Carter, Paddy DeMarco, Beau Jack, Tony Janiro, Lew Jenkins, Bob Montgomery, Archie Moore, Sandy Saddler and Ike Williams.

What follows are some of the better postwar battles. Nathan Mann had a hard-fought points victory over John Thomas at the Arena in New Haven on October 7, 1946. Hitting the canvas four times, Tony Falco of Middletown managed to draw Bob Pryor at the Auditorium in Hartford on January 7, 1947. Waterbury's Tony Ciarlo took a challenging victory at home over Frankie Vigeant in the Armory on March 21, 1947. Eddie Compo picked up an outstanding local victory at the Arena in New Haven by defeating the always tough Phil Terranova. Hartford's George Dunn put on an outstanding performance on November 10, 1948, when he picked up a victory over rival Teddy "Red Top" Davis. And Fairfield's Bernie Reynolds fought a challenging draw over rival and North Haven–born Ted Lowry in New Haven on November 14, 1949.

1950–59

Following nothing short of an incredible decade for boxing in Connecticut, the bottom dropped out in January 1950. The frequency of professional boxing matches in the state decreased by about 75 percent. The National Boxing Association blamed television for the alarming decline in attendance at boxing shows; others blamed the lack of quality fighters. The reality was that the IBC, formed by James D. Norris and Arthur M. Wirtz, engaged in a strategy to monopolize professional boxing. Buying out an ill Mike Jacobs and taking control of fighters under the command of Joe Louis gave the organization jurisdiction of several major arenas and essentially all but two weight divisions. From 1949 to 1955, all but two championship fights took place under their dominance. They also secured exclusive television contracts for twice-weekly fights at the Garden. This scenario left Connecticut matchmakers with their hands tied. They could not make the matches Connecticut fight fans wanted to see.

Since the boxing talent that folks, including Jack Dempsey, thought would emerge following World War II didn't exactly meet promoter expectations, the fight game would have to accept the few good fighters they had at their disposal while nurturing the stars of tomorrow. Connecticut, in far better shape than other states, had boxers like Larry Boardman (Marlborough), Dennis Patrick Brady (Hartford), Vic Cardell (Hartford), Johnny Cesario (Hartford), Eddie Compo (Johnny's younger brother, New Haven), Teddy "Red Top" Davis (Hartford), Billy Lynch (Hartford,) Carey Mace (Hartford) and Chico Vejar (Stamford), to note a few.

Lightweight Larry Boardman, the son of Sam Boardman, a journeyman fighter from the 1940s, turned pro in 1952. In 1956, his breakout year, he defeated four world champions: Wallace "Bud" Smith, Sandy Saddler, Paddy DeMarco and Jimmy Carter. And by the end of that year, he was ranked as the number-two lightweight contender of the world. Three consecutive losses the following year moved him off course, and he finally hung up the gloves in 1963.[74]

A prolific lightweight from the Catholic Youth Organization (CYO) ranks, Irish-proud Denis J. Brady, aka Dennis Patrick Brady, turned pro in 1944. Battling out of Hartford, the Bronx-born boxer didn't take his first loss until January 29, 1946 (Victor Flores). And, by 1950, the "Iron Chin" had shared a ring with Sal Bartolo, Vince Dell'Orto, Buddy Hayes, Freddie Russo and Sandy Saddler.[75] He retired from the ring in 1956.[76]

Fighting out of Hartford, southpaw Vic Cardelli, aka Vic Cardell, began his professional career in 1947. A mere two years later, he captured the Connecticut State Welterweight title with a twelve-round points victory over Frankie Vigeant. Cardell was durable, with a powerful left hook. It was during this year that many Connecticut fight fans recall his fierce rivalry with Waterbury welter Tommy Ciarlo. Between November 1949 and April 1950, the pair clashed four times, Cardell taking two, losing one and drawing. And it was in 1950 that Cardell posted consecutive victories over Aldo Minelli, Don Williams, Carmen Basilio, Jimmy Herring and Tony Cimmino, the latter four victories occurring inside Madison Square Garden. On *Gillette Friday Night Fights*, February 8, 1952, on the Garden undercard of the Chico Vejar / Johnny DeFazio battle, Cardell completely flattened Carmine Fiore in the seventh round of the eight-round semifinal. It was his best fight in the final three years of his career.

Hailing from New Haven, Eddie Campagnuolo, aka Eddie Compo, boxed for a span of eleven years while compiling an impressive record of 75-10-4. During the first five years of his career, having logged victories over Joey Iannotti, Joey Fontana, Phil Terranova and Teddy Davis, he was virtually unstoppable. On September 20, 1949, at Municipal Stadium in Waterbury, Compo fought for the world featherweight title against Willie Pep. In front of over ten thousand fight fans, the elite boxer dropped Compo twice in the fifth round and a final time in the seventh. With both eyes closed, the courageous Compo needed to be assisted to his dressing room. He fought the final round unable to even see Pep.

Known by many Nutmegers as a prime sparring partner for featherweight champion Willie Pep, Teddy "Red Top" Davis doesn't get enough credit for being an outstanding feather/lightweight. Granted, he took back-to-back losses to Pep in 1948 at the Auditorium Outdoor Arena in Hartford, but he would be the first to remind you that Pep had a few bouts under his belt. Fighting from 1946 until 1960, Davis appeared in over 150 fights and held victories over Jimmy McAlister, Julie Kogon, Paddy DeMarco and Percy Bassett.

Billy Lynch was a Bridgeport-born boxer with natural athletic ability. Noted for his quickness and accurate punching, he turned pro in 1953. Winning twelve consecutive bouts, his managers (Lenny Marello, Johnny Datro and San Gulino) hoped to take him to the top of the welterweight ranks. By 1961, Lynch had compiled a record of 42-3-0 and was fighting inside Madison Square Garden. Having taken victories over Luther Rawlings, Federico Plummer and Charley Tombstone Smith, he added Ted Wright to his list victims following his first Garden appearance. A bit of a showboat in the ring, Lynch, with that dangerous knockout punch of his, antagonized his opponents with hopes of bringing them into range. And it worked; more than half of his career victories were by knockout.[77]

A solid Hartford welterweight, Carey Mace fought from 1945 until 1962. Perfecting his skills on tomato cans until the summer of 1947, he started compiling some impressive victories. By the time he fought and defeated Joey Giardello on May 17, 1950, at St. Nicholas Arena in New York, he had taken wins over Rolly Johns, Sal DiMartino and Baby Tiger Flowers.[78]

Charming, articulate and a ring craftsman, Francis "Chico" Vejar, who studied dramatic arts at New York University, was a skillful boxer, long on style but short on punching power. In a career that spanned eleven years, he compiled a record of 92-20-4. Fighting some of the best-known welterweights and middleweights—among them champions Tony DeMarco, Gene Fullmer, "Kid" Gavilan, Joey Giardello and "Tiger" Jones, not to mention Carmen Fiore, Chuck Davey and Billy Graham—he retired at the young age of twenty-nine. Although he never won a title, his popularity, thanks to *Gillette Friday Night Fights*, led to two movie roles during the era.[79]

Also making a ring appearance in Connecticut in this decade were Paddy DeMarco, Tony DeMarco, "Kid" Gavilan, Joey Giardello, Billy Graham, Rocky Graziano, Beau Jack, Harold Johnson, Rocky Marciano, Floyd Patterson, Sugar Ray Robinson and Sandy Saddler.

There were other notable contests. Teddy Davis picked up a ten-round victory over a determined George Dunn at the Auditorium in Hartford on July 11, 1950. Stamford boxer Sammy Giuliani, having floored Roger Donaghue in the third round, somehow managed to hold off the fighter until the eighth round to take a victory. In one of those "I can't believe it's already over" battles,

Pittsburgh's Bill Bossio took out Bridgeport's Jimmy Rooney at the 2:11 mark of the opening round. The battle took place at Mitchell Field in Stamford on July 23, 1951. Hartford's Edward Oliveira, aka Eddie Oliver, slugged it out against Jackie Weber for eight rounds to a draw. The fight happened on July 10, 1952, at Hedges Stadium in Bridgeport. And Larry Boardman was unrelenting as he hammered Dennis Pat Brady over nearly ten rounds before grabbing a TKO victory at the 1:03 mark of the final round. It happened on November 1, 1955, at the State Theatre in Hartford.

Finally, when Vic Cardell, state welterweight champion, met California fighter Elmer Beltz at the Auditorium in Hartford on October 10, 1950, nobody was taking the fight too seriously. Granted, it opened the indoor professional season, but Beltz, a transplant from Los Angeles, was certainly no match, most fight fans believed, for Vic Cardell in his hometown. But they were wrong. A slow starter, Beltz, who was 20-3-1 at the time, finally woke up in the sixth

Elite boxer Leonardo Liotta, aka Tony DeMarco, grew up in the North End neighborhood of Boston. Recalled in Connecticut for his terrific trilogy against Gaspar Ortega, DeMarco managed to win their final battle, which took place in Boston.

round and carried the fight through the ninth. Incidentally, up to that point, the momentum had shifted back and forth. Beltz was far more accurate, but Cardell was a harder puncher. Both fighters were relentless in their pursuit and had the crowd on their feet for most of the bout. Entering the last round, Cardell, still shocked by what he had encountered, suddenly feared that he hadn't taken enough rounds—which was exactly the case. Taking a page from the Battalino playbook, Cardell exploded from his corner and tore into Beltz as if his life depended on it—certainly the decision did. Referee Joe Currie, impressed but not overwhelmed with Cardell's wake-up call, called it a draw. You never saw a fighter so happy for a stalemate as Cardell was that evening.

1960–65

The sixties marked the worst decade in in the history of professional boxing in Connecticut. At least as it pertained to the twentieth century. The annual frequency of professional fights in the state hit an all-time low. To put it in perspective, there were more fights in the year 1900 than there were in this entire decade.

In 1960, the Senate Subcommittee on Antitrust and Monopoly, chaired by Senator Estes Kefauver, held hearings into organized crime and professional boxing. The findings made by the subcommittee were not good. Also in 1960, the intimidating Sonny Liston, shadowed by underworld connections, became the number-one contender for the world heavyweight championship. The handlers of the current titleholder, Floyd Patterson, refused to give him a title shot because of his links to organized crime. While ring deaths weren't unusual to the sport, a couple of visible incidents began to drive the nail into the coffin of the semi-sweet science. On March 24, 1962, Benny Paret went twelve rounds against Emile Griffith. The fight ended when Paret went into a coma after being punched twenty-nine consecutive times. He died in the hospital ten days later. And on March 21, 1963, the immensely popular Davey Moore, having sustained a volley of punches by his opponent, "Sugar" Ramos, somehow managed to finish his fight but later died from his injuries. Soon, the public no longer had a taste for pugilism. Both professional and amateur boxing were outlawed in 1965 by act of the Connecticut State General Assembly.

Adding to the remorse felt by so many was the death of Augustine M. "Gus" Browne (1890–1962), the former matchmaker for the Hartford Boxing Club. Drawn from New York to Hartford in 1943 thanks to a bit of prompting by Lou Viscusi, Browne brought what talent he could during an exceedingly difficult time for the sport. His skills, contacts and instincts were priceless. As hard as it was to admit, it appeared as if the old school of Connecticut boxing was closing its doors without a new school to take its place.

1973–79

Despite the loss of three years of professional boxing, the 1970s managed to more than double the fight frequency of the previous decade. Considering all the obstacles that needed to be overcome, it was an impressive first step toward revitalizing the sport.

Following high school, Manuel "Manny" M. Leibert attended the University of Connecticut (then known as Connecticut State College), graduating in 1935. After obtaining his juris doctorate from Boston University School of Law in 1938, he served in the U.S. Air Force. Leibert's sport of passion was boxing. He was an experienced manager, promoter, trainer and second. And, as a founder of the Connecticut Boxing Guild, he was key in bringing the sport back to the state in 1973. It had been banned in Connecticut for eight years.

As if fate had intervened, the first license to promote boxing in the state since the sport had been reinstated was given to Manny Leibert on February 22, 1973. And receiving a referee's license was Al Couture, the former welterweight and first vice-president of the World Boxing Association.[80] With no fighters around and no place to hold a contest, both licensees had their hands full attempting to resurrect the sport. As far as fighters were concerned, Johnny Duke's boys (Bellevue Square Boys Club), or the largest contingent of area pugilists, were under the AAU (Amateur Athletic Union) umbrella. It was going to take some time, as Leibert, among others, understood, to load the pug pipeline in order to feed professional promotions. Meanwhile, finding a venue took center stage. The old Arena was gone, and Foot Guard Hall was no longer available. One option was the Hartford Civic Center, which broke ground on April 2, 1971, and hoped to be completed in late 1974. It wouldn't open until January 9, 1975.

Few recall the details of how Larry Butler of Lewiston, Maine, successfully defended his New England Welterweight title against Angel Torres of Pawtucket, Rhode Island, but many remember its significance as the first legalized Connecticut boxing show in nearly a decade. It happened inside the Hartford Hilton Ballroom on August 7, 1973. Among the five hundred in attendance was Barbara Dunn, boxing commissioner by virtue of being head of the Department of Consumer Protection. It wasn't always pretty, but promoter Billy Kowalczyk's maiden effort made history.

What follows are descriptions of a few of the battles that helped kick-start Connecticut's return to boxing. Light heavyweight Kevin Pentalow of New Britain captured a tough eight-round points victory over undefeated hometown boxer Greg Osowiecki at the State Armory in Waterbury on January 19, 1974. Brooklyn's Vito Antuofermo, the world's third-ranked middleweight, took a ten-round unanimous decision over an undefeated David Huckaby of Somers at the Bristol Arena on March 20, 1975. To Huckaby's credit, he withstood fifteen incredible shots to the head and body from his antagonist in the eighth round. John Dino Denis of Attleboro, Massachusetts, grabbed a sixth-round TKO victory over Jimmy Cross of Memphis, Tennessee, at the Hamden Sports Center on June 27, 1975. Dick Eklund, half brother of boxer Micky

Ward, grabbed an eight-round unanimous decision over Rufus Miller of Paterson, New Jersey, at East Hartford High School on October 30, 1976. And Canadian Johnny Summerhays grabbed a decisive victory over hometown fighter Vinnie DeBarros at the State Armory in Waterbury on November 6, 1976.[81]

SIGHTS & SOUNDS, JUNE 10, 1977

Sugar Ray Leonard competed from 1977 to 1997, winning world titles in five weight divisions. He fought twice in Connecticut, first at the Civic Center (1977, Hartford), followed later in a battle at Veterans Memorial Coliseum (1978, New Haven).

Billed as "Sights & Sounds," it was one of the finest evenings in Connecticut boxing history. The main event saw Olympian Sugar Ray Leonard capture an impressive TKO victory over New England Lightweight champion Vinnie DeBarros at the Civic Center in Hartford. With his words and action, Leonard taunted the hometown boxer before pinning him against the ropes in the third round and unleashing a damaging series of combinations. The end came at the 1:59 mark of the term. The ten-round semifinal saw Marvin Hagler of Brockton, Massachusetts, deliver a third-round knockout of Roy Jones. With the victory, Hagler hoped to position himself for a shot at middleweight champion Carlos Monzon. The undercard also saw Johnny Warr defeat Matt Robinson over six rounds; Curtis Smith, Leonard's sparring partner, knocked out Steve Snow of Holyoke in the second round; Ed Vigliotto of Milford drew Fred Fernandez of Brockton; and Odell Leonard, Sugar Ray's cousin, took a six-round decision over East Hartford's Johnny Harris. Over six thousand fight fans left the venue at 1 Civic Center Plaza in downtown Hartford, certain that they had just witnessed something special.[82]

1980–89

The 1980s, or the first full decade of Connecticut professional boxing since the 1950s, saw about a 50 percent improvement over the fight frequency of the previous decade. More important, some outstanding talent, the seeds of which had been sown during the previous decade, were beginning to bear fruit.

Born and raised in Hartford, Marlon Starling was precisely what professional boxing in Connecticut needed at this juncture: an unstoppable, charming and talented welterweight. Turning pro in 1979, Starling lost a fifteen-round unanimous decision to WBA/IBF welterweight Donald Curry on February 4, 1984; took an eleventh-round TKO victory over Golden Gloves legend Mark Breland to win the WBA welterweight title on August 22, 1987; fought a controversial no contest (initially deemed a loss) against Tomas Molinares on July 29, 1988; and, on February 4, 1989, knocked out Lloyd Honeyghan in the ninth round to win the Lineal/WBC welterweight title.[83]

Proof that the Connecticut boxing pipeline was filled with extraordinary talent, Marlon Starling was followed by Tyrone Booze, Luigi Camputaro, Sean Malone Jr., John Scully and Troy Wortham.

Hartford-born Tyrone Booze was a talented cruiserweight who began his professional career in 1982. Fifteen fights later, with a record of 10-3-2, he was battling undefeated Olympic bronze medalist Evander Holyfield. The future heavyweight champion had Booze reeling on the ropes in the sixth but couldn't put him away. Following the Holyfield skirmish, Booze fought Bert Cooper (1986), Henry Tillman (1986), Johnny du Plooy (1987) and Dwight Muhammad Qwai (1989). With a career record of 22-12-2, he hung up the gloves in 1998.

Born in Italy, Luigi Camputaro was more than happy to call Hartford one of his homes. Beginning his professional career by beating Felix Rodriguez in the old Agora Ballroom in West Hartford on June 19, 1984, "Little Luigi," aka "Kid Dynamite," aka the "Godfather," was a flyweight craftsman. Packing machine-gun combinations, he took undefeated elite fighter Johnny Tapia fifteen rounds in a losing effort. Camputaro won the Italian flyweight title (1986) and the vacant EBU European flyweight title (1993) before retiring from the ring in 1997.

With a father who was a talented trainer, manager, judge, referee and promoter in Connecticut, it was no surprise that Sean Malone Jr. found solace in a boxing ring. And it was under his father's guidance that the southpaw super lightweight polished his skills in Wallingford before making his professional debut in 1988. A mere seventeen bouts later, Malone, with a record of 15-2-0, captured the New England light welterweight title with a third-round TKO of Greg Cadiz. Often recalled for his hard-fought losing effort against David Santos for the NABF super light title, Malone left the ring in 1998 with a record of 23-6.

Concluding an outstanding amateur career, John Scully, aka the "Iceman," turned professional in 1988. Simply tenacious in the ring, Scully quickly refined his skills. Finishing the decade with an impressive victory over the undefeated Billy Bridges, he entered the 1990s with an intimidating record of 18-1. Following two heartfelt losses against two outstanding boxers—the first to Michael Nunn for the inaugural NABO super middleweight on December 8, 1995, and the second against Henry Maske for the IBF light heavyweight title—Scully could have padded his record with victories over tomato cans, but he didn't. Following his defeat against Maske, Scully never met another fighter with a losing record and finished his outstanding career at 38-11.

A professional boxer who also attended the University of Hartford, Troy Wortham, aka "Schoolboy," was as interested in his education as he was his boxing prowess. But it depended on exactly when you happened to catch him as to which one took precedence. Beginning his professional career by knocking out Larry Smith in the opening round on June 5, 1982, Wortham remained undefeated (24-0) at the end of 1985. On January 25, 1986, he found himself facing Golden Gloves legend Mark Breland in Lancaster, Pennsylvania. Despite being knocked down twice during the ten-round battle, he managed to take the loss standing up. Following a sixth-round TKO loss to Julio Cesar Vasquez at Caesars Palace in Las Vegas, Wortham concluded his career with an impressive record of 29-2.

A few nice battles seemed to slip between the cracks. Roger Leonard, Sugar Ray's older brother and the world's fourth-ranked junior middleweight, was shocked when he was stopped (TKO) during the tenth and final round by Jersey fighter Mario Maldonado. It happened on February 9, 1981, at the Civic Center in Hartford. Joe Louis Manley knocked out defending IBF junior welterweight champion Gary Hinton, who had hit the canvas in the second round, at the 2:14 mark of the tenth round. The fight took place at the Civic Center on October 30, 1986. Elite boxer Julian Jackson came to town and defeated Hartford boxer Milton "Cuda" Leaks by TKO at the 0:38 mark of the tenth round. The battle, which was for the WBC Continental Americas junior middleweight championship, saw Jackson down (in truth, a slip) in the sixth round. Finally, Leon Spinks, Olympic gold medalist and a boxer who dethroned Muhammad Ali, was knocked out at 0:33 of the opening round of his bout against Tony Morrison. The fight took place at the Trumbull Marriott on May 30, 1988. Morrison was a replacement for boxer Phil Brown.

1990–92

The 1990s saw little improvement in professional fight frequency from the previous decade. While the first four years of the decade (1990–93) reflected one of the worst periods of the century, the latter four years (1996–99) marked a noticeable improvement over the previous thirty. This was courtesy of a market transition. Casino boxing was the springboard needed to catapult professional boxing in Connecticut back to the forefront. And it did precisely that.

Carrying professional boxing into the next decade, not to mention the next century, was a talented group of fighters: lightweight Israel "Pito" Cardona (Hartford), heavyweight Lawrence Clay Bey (Hartford), light heavyweight Eric Harding (West Hartford), super welterweight Delvin Rodriguez (Danbury), middleweight Travis Simms (Norwalk) and featherweight Angel Vazquez (Hartford).

A bit later, other noteworthy boxers followed: light heavyweight "Bad" Chad Dawson (New Haven), light heavyweight Charles Foster (New Haven), heavyweight Tony Grano (Hebron), super lightweight Anthony Laureano (East Hartford), featherweight Mike Oliver (Hartford), super featherweight Matt Remillard (Hartford), super bantamweight Luis Rosa (New Haven), featherweight Shelly Vincent (New London) and super welterweight Jimmy Williams (New Haven), to name a few.

While space doesn't allow for details regarding all of the great battles these gladiators fought, at least we can acknowledge their incredible contribution.

Chapter Eleven

THE FIGHT GAME

OUTSIDE THE ROPES

*Keep away from people who try to belittle your ambitions. Small people always do
that, but the really great make you feel that you too can become great.*
—Mark Twain

Every successful professional boxer relies on a team of talented individuals
to not only elevate him or her to the pinnacle of their craft, but also to
keep them there. Blessed to have talent both inside and outside the ropes,
boxing in Connecticut has thrived. A plethora of extraordinary individuals
has provided the knowledge and inspiration, organization and resources,
safety and protection, evaluation and judgment and observation and
assessment.

KNOWLEDGE AND INSPIRATION

Leadership of the team belongs to the boxing manager. This individual
assembles the components necessary to achieve success. As the boxer's mentor
and advisor, the manager sets the course toward the ultimate goal and keeps
it on track. As the captain of the ship, a boxing manager takes control of the
speed at which his fighter will travel—in other words, opponent selection,
weight class and fight length, not to mention many other duties. Without a
boxing manager, a fighter doesn't know which way to turn; after all, if you
don't know where you are going, any road will take you there.

A boxing coach, or trainer, has the responsibility of maximizing the mental and physical skills of a fighter. The coach's greatest assets are knowledge and inspiration. Be it the development of a new boxer or assistance to an experienced fighter, they guarantee the condition of the product that enters the ring. In automobile racing, a crew chief has a similar role.

As a legal scholar and public defender, Arnold "Arnie" Bayer forged a terrific friendship with Julio Gallucci, aka Johnny Duke, boxing manager and director of the Bellevue Square Boys Club (BSBC) in the North End of Hartford. Sharing a passion for the sweet science, the pair assisted in the development of both amateur and professional pugilists, most notably "Superb" Herb Darity and Hector "Cuchi" Ortiz.

From 1933 to 1937, Walter J. "Wally" Bonola was the state amateur middleweight boxing champion. But it was his role as the thirteen-year owner and operator of Wally Bonola's Restaurant on Church Street in New Britain that brought him the greatest satisfaction.[84] The former professional prizefighter loved talking with friends about the sweet science. Be it as a boys' boxing coach or as a manager in the Joseph Walicki Jr. baseball Little League, Bonola was admired and an inspiration to many.

One of Connecticut's most flamboyant criminal defense lawyers, F. Mac Buckley also had a love of the ring. Perhaps best known for training and managing Marlon Starling, a world welterweight champion, he also worked with several New England champions and many amateur contenders out of the Charter Oak Gym in Hartford.

Having been drawn to the ring early in life, Val Callahan became a manager, trainer and second long before he considered promotion. Working with Connecticut pugilists such as Wallingford welterweight Tracy Ferguson, the Kaplan brothers, Wallingford welter Sheik Johnny Leonard, Meriden feather Georgie Lynch and Meriden feather Jackie Pilkington, he crafted his skills prior to conducting the boxing affairs of the Silver City Athletic Club.

A gifted fighter, arbiter, advisor and coach, Hartford native Johnny Callas found his passion both in and outside the ring. As part of the nationally ranked Central Connecticut State University (National Collegiate Boxing Association) boxing program, under his mentor Billy Taylor, he captured a national championship and was a three-time All-American; consequently, he even represented the United States in international competition. A professional referee since 1994, Callas has officiated nearly three hundred

This display case, located inside the Connecticut Boxing Hall of Fame, is dedicated to Marlon Starling. It includes his used robe and trunks, training gloves and a photo of the fighter with F. Mac Buckley.

bouts, including the Miguel Cotto / Muhammad Abdullayev WBO light welterweight title at Madison Square Garden (2005). As founder and executive director of the Charter Oak Boxing Academy, he has been nationally recognized by boxing periodicals such as *The Ring* and organizations such as the World Boxing Council (2011 WBC Hero). Beloved by his students, "Coach" Callas carries the patina of enthusiasm and ring excellence wherever he travels.

Speaking of being venerated as a coach and a mentor, take Paul Cichon. The boxing director of the Manchester Ring of Champions Society has trained numerous national titleholders, including Miguel Ayala, Matt Remillard and Mykquan Williams. Growing up in his native Holyoke, Cichon got hooked on the sweet science and never looked back. As the director of the Manchester Police Athletic League (PAL) boxing program, he instilled discipline while revitalizing the curriculum. He even got himself inducted into the Manchester Sports Hall of Fame in 2008. Cichon was also inducted into the New England Golden Gloves Hall of Fame in 2000.

It took Brian Clark, who picked up boxing in the navy, to transform one of New Haven's once most dangerous neighborhoods into a sanctuary for pugilism. Known as Ring One Boxing Gym—one of the oldest continuously operating institutions of its kind in Connecticut—it has become an institution. Located on Congress Avenue, Ring One has been essentially a one-man operation and a nonprofit labor of love since its inception. More than merely a perfectionist, Clark, who in recent years has worked with Tramaine "Midget" Williams and "Bad" Chad Dawson, exudes both determination and dedication.

Marlon Starling (world welterweight champion), Lawrence Clay-Bey (1996 U.S. Olympic team), Jimmy Blythe (two-time national champion), Herbie Cox, Herb Darity, Kelvin Anderson and Donny Nelson all shared a common denominator: they all trained with Desi Clark. Forever humble, Clark, who ducked praise and seldom countered criticism, found solace in his discreet role.

The San Juan Center, over on Main Street in Hartford, began as a youth facility when it opened in 1992. But it wasn't long before it became the capital's premier cabbage patch for both hopeful professional and promising amateur fighters. Similar to Stillman's Gym in New York, it drew trainers, and even those who thought they were, searching for a meal ticket. Boxing director George Cruz, often assisted by chief trainer Angel Vazquez Sr., oversaw activities at the gym. In addition to being in Marlon Starling's corner when he won the WBA welterweight title in 1987, Cruz has assisted other fighters, including Eric Harding, Angel Vazquez Jr. and John Scully, along with referees Michael Ortega and Danny Schiavone.

Bill Lee, the sports editor for the *Hartford Courant*, often referred to Bill Gore as the best boxing trainer and handler in the business. And why not? Gore trained Willie Pep, from before he captured the world featherweight title until almost the end of the legendary boxer's career. Also recalled for his early years spent with light heavyweight champion Mike McTigue, Gore later used his skills to craft Melio Bettina into championship form. When the trainer teamed up with Lou Viscusi, it was an unbeatable combination.[85]

Founding the Norwalk-based John Harris Boxing Club, the man himself trained three world champions under its roof. It was back in Cleveland, as a teenager, that John Harris was drawn to the ring. The former Golden Gloves boxer put nearly sixty bouts under his belt before turning professional. A loss in his debut battle convinced Harris that if he wanted to stay close to the sport, perhaps it was best to stay outside of the ropes. Settling in Norwalk, he teamed with former pro boxer Ted Lowry to establish the NEON Boxing Club. And a year later, he started the Meadow Gardens Boxing Club, later to become the John Harris Boxing Club, in South Norwalk. Working with fighters Fred Kitt, Travis Simms and his twin brother, Tarvis, was a testament to the acute skills of John Harris.

As a former New England lightweight boxing champion, Mosey King had no idea that when he became an assistant boxing coach at Yale in 1906, he had found his life's calling. Succeeding head coach Bill Dole, the New York–born pugilist served as head coach for forty-six years. Adamant about preserving the integrity of the fight game, King was also Connecticut's first boxing commissioner, serving from 1921 to 1923.

To say professional boxing owes a debt of gratitude to Manuel M. "Manny" Leibert would be similar to saying that the state of Connecticut owes the same to Jonathan Trumbull. There are simply times in history when the right person comes along at the right time. Although a legal scholar and successful entrepreneur, not to mention an air force veteran, Leibert was happiest around a boxing ring, as not only a second, but also as a trainer, manager and promoter. He loved the sweet science. As a founder of the Connecticut Boxing Guild, Leibert recognized the significance of the fight game and those who contributed to it. He was pivotal in revitalizing Connecticut boxing in 1973, and there is not a fight fan in the state who doesn't cherish his legacy.

If your name was Malone, and you happened to be from Wallingford, life probably took place in or around a boxing ring. Irish-born Sean D.

Malone Sr. was self-taught in the sweet science and trained fighters on both the amateur and professional levels. After assisting the Police Athletic League (PAL) boxing program in his hometown, he operated Malone's Gym in Wallingford. It was from there that his son Sean Malone Jr. began his successful boxing career. His love of boxing was matched only by his love of family and baseball. Of the latter, it was as a coach for the Wallingford Little League that the patriarch took his team to the finals in the Little League World Series of 1979.

As an amateur boxer, Orlando Montalvo competed in 125 fights, winning 110 of them. For many pugilists in Puerto Rico, that would be satisfaction enough. However, Montalvo, following a brief professional career, settled in Stamford. And, it's from there that the talented pugilist, a former Roberto Duran sparring partner, ended up operating Montalvo Boxing Gym.

Roland Pier-Federici grew up on the streets of New London. His interest in boxing came courtesy of a Mississippi pistol-whipping that he never forgot. Having dabbled in the sweet science, the incident prompted him to get serious. As an amateur welterweight, he lost more fights than he won, but it never seemed to bother him much; he often stated that he was late bloomer who never bloomed. This was because he fell in love with training. Never far from a gym, Pier trained all over the world. And, thanks to sports, six colleges and a decade-long commitment, he finally received his degree in education. For twenty-eight years, he taught the fifth grade in Ledyard by day and trained boxers by night.

Born in New York City, Charles Francis Pilkington learned to box by watching the fighters in his neighborhood gym. That in itself isn't unique, until you attach names like Benny Leonard, Harlem Tommy Murphy and Irish Patsy Cline to the situation. Realizing that he had some potential, the featherweight refined his skills as an amateur before turning pro in 1919. By 1920, Pilkington was battling out of Waterbury and Meriden against fighters such as Meriden's Young Tony Caponi, Waterbury's Johnny Shugrue and New Jersey's Willie Herman. Hanging up the gloves in 1925, after compiling a record of 23-11-7, he became a noted referee, matchmaker, trainer and promoter. He is often recalled for his work with Kid Kaplan and Eddie Compo.

A semiprofessional and briefly professional boxer, Joseph Rocco Rossi heard his country call, and he answered. Following his enlistment and service in the U.S. Army, Rossi, unsure in which direction to turn, assisted Joe Triano with the YMCA's youth boxing program. Later, he formed the Rossi Boxing Club at the Naugatuck YMCA, where he mentored young men and women in the fine art of self-defense.

This framed 1988 fight poster, located inside the Connecticut Boxing Hall of Fame, includes the images of (*left to right*) Angel Gonzalez, "Irish" Sean Malone, "Gentleman" John Scully, Troy "Schoolboy" Wortham and "Irish" John Fortin.

In 1933, Bridgeport's George John "Pop" Russo was turning heads as a powerful lightweight. Compiling a record of 27-20-3 and boxing in venues such as Fenway Park, Boston Garden and Walnut Beach Stadium, he captured victories over Al Gillette, Roland LeCuyer and Joey Zodda. Later, he turned to training and operated gyms such as Red Man's Hall, the Acorn Club and East Washington Avenue Gym. Perhaps best known for the many dedicated years of service and pleasure teaching boxing at Bridgeport PAL Boxing Gym, Russo inspired many.

As a decorated amateur and skilled professional boxer, John Scully excelled at his trade. After reading a book about Muhammad Ali (*The Greatest: My Own Story*), he knew precisely what he wanted to do with his life. And, when John Scully makes a decision, he sticks with it; he has never had a middle ground. Talented and inspiring, Scully turned his attention to training. Although some view developing champions and motivating youngsters to live a clean and healthy life as demanding, Scully, thankfully, in the hearts of his pupils, views it as his calling.

Catching the boxing bug during his senior year at Naugatuck High School, Joseph C. Triano, like many, graduated before serving his country in the U.S.

Army. It was while serving that he captured the middleweight championship of Australia and the Southwest Pacific. Returning home, Triano found his vocation as a boxing instructor at the YMCA.

Born in Schenectady and raised in Tampa, Lou Viscusi moved to Hartford in 1929. Although he was a talented promoter, it was as a boxing manager that he made his mark—specifically, handling the careers of welterweight Del Flanagan, heavyweight Roy Harris, middleweight Tony Licata, welterweight Manny Gonzalez, heavyweight Cleveland Williams and featherweight Willie Pep. In addition to Pep, he also assisted Joe Brown and Bob Foster to world championships. He partnered with Bill Gore, and the duo formed one of the most significant teams in boxing history. They handled the careers of hundreds of fighters trying desperately to contend for a title.

Connecticut has seen so many gifted boxing trainers and coaches over the years that it's impossible to name everyone, but a few others should be noted: fighter and manager Don Angell; (Kogon) boxing manager Jack Bluman; fight manager Sam Boardman; trainer Walter Brown; trainer John Datro; (Yale) boxing coach Bill Dole; (Battalino) fight manager Hy Malley; (Coast Guard Academy) trainer Mickey McClernon; (Battalino) fight manager Lenny Marello; coach Tony Nelson; trainer Pepe Vazquez and motivator Sammy "Suave" Vega.

ORGANIZATION AND RESOURCES

Putting their money where their mouths are, boxing promoters are responsible for every element of a boxing match. They assume all of the financial risk associated with an event and spend hours making sure that a promotion runs smoothly. Guaranteeing that a production meets a customer's satisfaction requires tremendous attention to detail. From designing, printing and distributing event posters, to even scaling the tickets, they understand that every element is critical to their success. Not only do they expect the unexpected, they also prepare for it.

AN OLD-SCHOOL GENTLEMAN, GUS Browne, who escaped New York City for the rolling hills of Connecticut, was beloved by everyone associated with Connecticut boxing. He trained and managed fighters "Irish" Patsy Cline, Denis "Pat" Brady and Vic Cardell, to name a few. Besides promoting shows in Hartford, he handled matches in upstate New York and eastern Pennsylvania.

Jimmy Burchfield at the podium during the press conference for NBC Sports Network's popular *Fight Night* TV series. The network's 2013 season began with a battle between Sergey Kovalev and Gabriel Campillo.

From cornerman and referee to international judge and promoter, it was a long road for Jimmy Burchfield. However, he has always welcomed the work. And, like a fighter taking that first punch, he has met every challenge like a champion. Be it his restaurant, Jimmy Burchfield's Classic, which was over on Charles Street, just over the line in North Providence, or his first promotion, in 1992 at the old Rocky Point Palladium, Burchfield fell in love with entertainment, which always included a boxing spin. Recognized for his relationship with fighters Vinny Pazienza and Chad Dawson, Burchfield currently runs Classic Entertainment & Sports, which has promoted boxing cards all over the country.[86]

After serving in World War II, John R. Burns Jr. joined the Hartford Police Department and retired thirty-six years later as a lieutenant. From supervisor for the Hartford Police Athletic League (PAL) boxing program to state director of boxing, his experience—not to mention his trademark smile—was always a welcome sight. Burns acted as an advisor to the Foxwoods and Mohegan Sun boxing commissions.

Joe DeGuardia followed in the footsteps of his father, Joe DeGuardia Sr. The elder's professional boxing career (1947–53) included battles against Carmine Fiore, Sammy Giuliani and Billy Murphy. So, when junior took an interest in the sweet science, it surprised few. Receiving his undergraduate degree from Fordham University and his graduate degree (juris doctorate) from Hofstra Law School, Joe also managed to squeeze in a bit of boxing. He won the welterweight division (147 pounds open division) of the 1988 New York City Golden Gloves tournament. In 1992, he founded Star Boxing, a boxing promotional company originally based in the Bronx. DeGuardia brought many exciting promotions to Connecticut.

A former head of boxing programming for HBO Sports, Louis John "Lou" Dibella created and orchestrated the highly successful series *Boxing After Dark*. As founder of Dibella Entertainment, based in New York, he has always had a soft spot for Connecticut and has brought quality baseball and boxing to the state.

From promoting shows with the Doors, the Who, Jimi Hendrix and Janis Joplin, Sheldon "Shelly" Finkel made a successful jump to boxing in 1980. Assisting amateur stars first, he helped frame the careers of many outstanding professional boxers, including Mike Tyson, Manny Pacquiao, Evander Holyfield, Pernell Whitaker, Meldrick Taylor, Mike McCallum and Alex Ramos. Finkel is often recalled for his promotion of the Mike Tyson / Michael Spinks fight on June 27, 1988. It doesn't surprise the promoter, as he managed the largest pay-per-view event up to that time.

Born in Guebwiller, France, Armand "Al" Weill moved to the United States at the age of thirteen. Taking an interest in dance, he became a professional ballroom dancer. Realizing that most of the venues he waltzed across also promoted dance competitions and boxing matches, Weill became manager at the Harlem Sporting Club. The first professional boxer he managed was New York State featherweight champion Charlie Pilkington, aka the "Meriden Flash." In 1930, Weill and Dick Gray teamed up to establish the Thames Arena in New London as a popular oasis for professional boxing. Later, Weill conducted promotions all across the state of Connecticut, most notably at Foot Guard Hall. Best known for managing heavyweight champion Rocky Marciano, Weill also managed world champions Lou Ambers, Marty Servo and Joey Archibald.

As the leading sports promoter in Connecticut in the early 1900s, George F. Mulligan operated professional boxing clubs in Hartford and Waterbury. He promoted three world championship matches: the 1919 bantamweight championship bout between Joe Lynch and Pete Herman at Waterbury; the

1925 featherweight championship match between Kid Kaplan and Babe Herman at Waterbury; and the 1926 feather title bout between Kid Kaplan and Bobby Garcia at Hartford. Mulligan was also the founder and owner of the Hartford Blues of the National Football League.

Support for Connecticut boxing and its legacy comes from many individuals, some recognized worldwide. Daryl Peoples, International Boxing Federation President, comes to mind. In 2010, he became only the fourth IBF president and chief executive officer, and he is considered by many to be the finest to ever hold the position.

In the early 1920s, Dominic J. "Pete" Perone decided to nurture some of the outstanding young boxing talent floating around Hartford by opening up the Charter Oak Athletic Club. Prior to that, he opened his first boxing gym on Windsor Street in Hartford, opposite the old State Theater. Perone, who also worked for G. Fox & Company and did a bit of vaudeville on the side, trained and developed pugs like Joe Howard, Johnny Duke, Graham Holmes, Bobby Ivy and Willie Pep, to name a few. Later, he hooked up with Ed Hurley, and the duo promoted amateur shows at Capitol Park and Foot Guard Hall. Perone was also the first president of the Connecticut Boxing Guild.[87]

He was the Hartford jeweler whose name and slogan—POMG, for "Peace of Mind Guaranteed"—became household words. William Myron "Bill" Savitt operated his jewelry store for nearly seven decades at 35 Asylum Street in Hartford. He formed the semipro Savitt Gems baseball team in the late 1920s, and quality baseball became his passion. Savitt was the owner of Bulkeley Stadium in the South End from 1932 to 1946. Not only did some of the greatest names in baseball come to town, but he also transformed Tuesday evenings into "Fight Night." Willie Pep fought four of his first five professional contests in the stadium, including his debut.

During the 1950s, Sam Silverman broke away from the International Boxing Club run by Jim Norris and Company in hopes of making a fresh start. But, trying to break the club's domination of the fight game was like melting a block of ice with a cigarette lighter. Yet, Silverman remained focused on his goals. Often remembered for matching the undefeated Rocky Marciano in thirty-two of his forty-nine bouts, Silverman also promoted twenty-five world championship bouts, along with shows featuring popular boxers Willie Pep, Phil Terranova and Harold "Chubby" Gomes.

Born in Italy, Vito Tallarita moved with his family to Enfield at the young age of seven. Taking an early interest in the fight game, he excelled as an amateur featherweight, twice battling Willie Pep, before trying his luck as a professional in 1940. But his professional aspirations quickly ran dry. And, thankfully so, as he was the matchmaker for Marlon Starling's first twenty professional bouts. Tallarita was also one of the figures involved in the elite career of Sugar Ray Leonard.

A natural athlete, Billy Taylor was a professional boxer, referee and coach. Spending three decades teaching in the Hartford school system, he also led his junior high basketball team to twelve city championships. Taylor coached the 1945 Coast Guard National Championship team, guided Central Connecticut for eight seasons in the 1980s and produced three national champions and thirty-two All-American boxers.

Connecticut boxing was revitalized in 1992 by the opening of Foxwoods Resort Casino and the efforts of Peter Timothy. As commissioner of the Mashantucket Pequot Tribal Nation from 1995 to 2009, he regulated hundreds of fights. Often recalled for two of the biggest fights at Foxwoods during his tenure—John Ruiz versus Evander Holyfield for the heavyweight title and James Toney versus Vasily Jurov for the cruiserweight championship—Timothy worked with many of the biggest names in the business.

Charles "Chick" Wergeles was born on the Lower East Side of New York. Hailing from a large family, he learned quickly to defend himself or starve to death. Having developed some printing knowledge, Wergeles moved to Bridgeport in 1917 and eventually opened a print shop. Always—or so most believed—having his hand in the fight business, he eventually landed back in New York. Along with Al Weill, he managed Rocky Marciano; Wergeles also managed Beau Jack. He promoted shows at Queensboro Stadium, White City Stadium (Savin Rock) and New Haven Arena. In the 1960s, he made a gallant effort to promote new boxing talent in both Hartford and Bridgeport.

As good as Connecticut organizations have been, acknowledging those who have contributed greatly to the manly art of self-defense, there are always some that slip between the cracks of history. Some of these overlooked people include Waterbury promoter Johnny Brickell; Bristol manager, matchmaker and promoter Thomas Hinchcliff; matchmaker at Olympic Athletic Club (1925) Ed Hurley; Bridgeport promoter Connie Lewis; and Hartford matchmaker Rocco Palotti. Digging a bit deeper, more names surface. Kid Kaplan met businessman Moe Levine at the Lenox Athletic Club. It was Levine, who dabbled in many things, including sports promoting, who introduced Kaplan to Dennis McMahon. Individuals like Levine are too often forgotten.

SAFETY AND PROTECTION

Ringside physicians play a dynamic and multifaceted role in combat sports. When boxers enter a ring, they want to know that they are safe. Injuries, often to the head, neck, face and hands, are common in boxing. Brain injury, both acute and chronic, is clearly the major risk. Ringside physicians are responsible for protecting both boxers. Since the task requires quick decisions, often based on a limited examination, an acute awareness of a possible problem has to be almost instinctive to the physician.

WHEN YOU THINK OF talented ring physicians in Connecticut, two come to mind: Dr. Anthony Alessi and Dr. Michael Schwartz. Both have been familiar figures at ringside for major fights at Mohegan Sun and Foxwoods Resort Casino.[88]

After eighteen years on the Mashantucket Pequot Tribal Council, including four as chairman, Kenny Reels was appointed to the Mashuntucket Pequot Gaming & Athletic Commission in 2009, where he oversaw the regulation of boxing and mixed martial arts (MMA). He was the perfect choice for many reasons, foremost being his love of the sport of boxing and his concern for a fighter's safety.

Barbara Dunn Fleming became the first woman to serve as Connecticut Commissioner of Consumer Protection, in 1971. In this capacity, she was also the boxing commissioner—the first woman to hold this position in the country.

EVALUATION AND JUDGMENT

The evaluation and judgment of a boxing match involves many individuals. Their responsibilities are clearly defined in a document, *State of Connecticut Regulation of the Department of Emergency Services and Public Protection concerning Boxing and Mixed Martial Arts.*[89]

It clearly states that, for each bout in the state of Connecticut, the following officials shall be in attendance: one referee, three judges, one announcer, at least one physician and two timekeepers.

As the sole arbiter of a boxing match, a referee plays a unique and specialized role in a contest. From instructing contestants and their chief seconds to determining the sportsmanship of the boxers, a referee guarantees a genuine and safe performance.

Judging a boxing match sounds simple. It is not. In all Connecticut boxing bouts, the judges use a ten-point must system. Points are awarded during a contest for clean punching, effective aggressiveness, ring generalship and defense.[90]

A POPULAR BOXING FIGURE in Connecticut because of his work as a judge, referee and head of the state's amateur organization for years, Lou Bogash Jr. served his country proudly during World War II and even managed a bit of boxing while in the U.S. Marine Corps. By 1987, he had already refereed over five thousand rounds, including collegiate tournaments. Employed by the Bridgeport Brass Company for thirty-seven years, where he worked in the security and safety department, Bogash was also employed at aircraft engine manufacturer AVCO Lycoming.

Although two decades had passed since Bat Battalino met Andre Routis of France in a featherweight championship battle at the East Hartford Velodrome, there stood the familiar face of boxing referee William "Billy" Conway, prepared to handle the featherweight title fight between Willie Pep and Eddie Compo at Waterbury. Conway was known for his integrity and sound judgment; if he was the third man in the ring, you knew the battle was on the level.

It was as a sportswriter that Glenn Feldman caught the boxing bug. And to satisfy his passion, he looked no further than ringside, and the seat designated for a boxing judge. As a distinguished adjudicator, Feldman's career has taken him all over the world; he once judged two world-title fights over two nights in two countries, England and the United States. As the driving force behind the Connecticut Boxing Hall of Fame, he has been essential in reviving interest in the state's rich pugilistic past.

Dick Flaherty knows boxing. In 1967, he started refereeing amateurs for the AAU (now USA Boxing) before turning his attention to the pro ranks. His first official appearance came on January 9, 1969, and he never looked back. On May 13, 1978, Flaherty garnered his first assignment involving an elite boxer, refereeing the battle between "Marvelous" Marvin Hagler and Kevin Finnegan at Boston Garden. His ring prowess has taken him to Asia, Europe, Canada, Mexico and numerous cities throughout the United States while working with boxers such as Ray Leonard, Dana Rosenblatt, Zab Judah, James Toney, Jesse James Leija, Chad Dawson and Vinny Pazienza, to name a few. Ironically, he is often recalled for his presence outside the ropes as a judge for the legendary

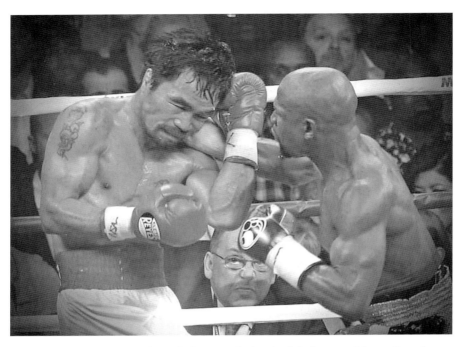

Judge Glenn Feldman peers through the ropes during the fight between Manny Pacquiao and Adrien Broner for the WBA welterweight championship on January 19, 2019, in Las Vegas, Nevada. *Photograph courtesy of Glenn Feldman.*

first fight between Arturo Gatti and Micky Ward, held at the Mohegan Sun Arena on May 18, 2002.

William E. Hutt attended Central Connecticut State University and the University of Hartford and graduated from the Connecticut School of Broadcasting. Employed by The Hartford for nearly three decades, he had a passion for boxing, in particular its history. Finding his calling outside the ring, Hutt became a professional boxing judge with the International Boxing Federation, the United States Boxing Association, the World Boxing Union and the North America Boxing Federation. Larry Holmes, Vinny Pazienza, Micky Ward, James Toney, Bernard Hopkins and Julio Cesar Chavez are a few of the outstanding boxers he had the opportunity to cast judgment on.

Born in West Virginia, John Duke Lawson spent his seventeenth birthday at Marine Corps boot camp in Parris Island, South Carolina. Following six years of active duty, he joined another force, the Waterbury Police Department. Leaving the detective ranks after twenty years, Lawson went on to become a fraud investigator for the Connecticut Department

Marlon Starling, Mary Anne Guarco and John Laudati during a ceremony at the Connecticut Boxing Hall of Fame.

of Labor. Complementing his business and family life was a love of the fight game. It was that fervor that drove Lawson to become a boxing official. Often noted for being the third man in the ring for the 1977 fight between Marvin Hagler and Roy Jones, he also judged fights involving Joe Calzaghe, Chad Dawson, Zab Judah and Antonio Tarver.[91]

Practicing primarily as a trial lawyer since 1981, John L. Laudati serves as president and legal counsel to the Connecticut Boxing Hall of Fame and chairs its giving committee. Integral to the organization meeting its mission of promoting the sport of boxing in this great state while assisting deserving members of the boxing community, he is admired for his dedication, precision and professionalism.

When you have a boxing legend like Gaspar Ortega as a father, it's hard to dodge the footsteps. But you can create your own, and Michael Ortega did precisely that. By the mid-1990s, Ortega was polishing his skills as a professional referee. Known worldwide for his ring expertise, he has worked with Joe Calzaghe, Vinny Pazienza, Johnny Tapia, Zab Judah, Nassem Hamed, Lucia Rijker and Paul Malignaggi, and those are only a few prior to

2003. Few realize that Michael Ortega was born during the seventh round of his father's battle with Kid Gavilan on October 27, 1957.

A Providence native and graduate of Brown University, Clark Sammartino was always drawn to the ring. As a boxing judge, his prolific career spanned from 1987 until 2017. The notable fighters he evaluated include Vinny Pazienza, Greg Haugen, Felix Trinidad, Tommy Morrison, Hector Camacho, Johnny Tapia, Naseem Hamed and Marco Antonio Barrera. An oral surgeon who loved sports, Sammartino was also a board member of Brown's Athletic Hall of Fame.

A boxing official for over twenty years, Don Trella always understood that a great boxing judge does his job and avoids controversy. More important, "he gets it right." It's every judge's greatest compliment, and it fits Trella like a glove. As an adolescent, he loved watching boxing with his father and grandfather, and he still relishes the stories he heard. It was Harold Lederman who steered the Mohegan Sun employee toward officiating, and he has been grateful ever since. Having judged over eight hundred professional bouts since 2002, the Connecticut native understands his craft from every angle, be it at a corner gym or a world championship fight. He and his good friend Glenn Feldman are the finest two judges in the fight game.

And there are many others worthy of note: Rebelle Carpenter, Bristol's deputy boxing commissioner; Judge Steve Epstein of New Britain; referee Ken Ezzo; referee Dave Fitzgerald of New Haven, who oversaw many rounds inside the Lenox Athletic Club as the twentieth century began; judge and former boxing writer George Smith of West Hartford; referee Steve Smoger of New Jersey / Windsor; and referee "Honest John" Willis.

OBSERVATION AND ASSESSMENT

As with judging, observation and assessment play an important role in the fight game. After all, where would the sport be today if it weren't for Don Dunphy, Red Barber and Graham McNamee? Viewers, especially during pay-for-view battles, rely on observation for an accurate performance evaluation. Let's face it, even in this age of high-definition television, following a Vasyl Lomachenko right jab from your couch isn't easy.

The dynamic nature and popularity of the fight game lends itself to comparison. How many times has each of us been asked the question: Who do you think was better…? In reality, few have the knowledge to even attempt an answer. Typically, those who do know are not the beat writers sitting ringside or the magazine men a row back, but dedicated historians with the skills to sort through promoter propaganda and ringside rhetoric.

STARTING AS A COPY boy in 1925, Joe Casano became a reporter for the *Hartford Times* as a teenager and rose to assistant sports editor. Born in Yonkers in 1908, he was raised in Bristol before moving to Hartford and then West Hartford. As a member of the Connecticut Sports Writers Alliance, the National Turf Writers Association and the Connecticut Boxing Guild, he loved sharing stories about the sweet science. He was also a correspondent for *The Ring*.

In 1929, while still a student at Wesleyan University in Middletown, Sam Cohen began pushing a pen as a sports correspondent for the *Hartford Courant*. Later, he applied his skills for the *Meriden Journal* (1932–47) and the *Bridgeport Sunday Herald* (1947–74). From 1974 to 1976, Cohen was executive secretary of the State of Connecticut Department of Consumer Protection's Athletic Division, where he had a chance to apply his vast knowledge of the sweet science. When he wasn't actively participating in a boxing event, Cohen was writing about it, be it for a trade, such as *The Ring*, or even a reference book, like the 1956 edition of *World Scope Encyclopedia and Yearbook*. In addition to being selected as the Connecticut Boxing Guild Man of the Year (1956), Cohen was also honored with the Arthur B. McGinley Memorial Award (1980) by the Connecticut Sports Writers' Alliance.

As sports editor of the *New Britain Herald*, Gerald P. "Jerry" Crean was a fixture in Connecticut boxing for as long as most could remember. As a decorated veteran of World War I—awarded three Purple Hearts for his heroic actions—Crean began his writing career in Plainville before heading to Southington, then on to New Britain. As president of the Connecticut Sportswriter Alliance, he was enormously popular and even served multiple terms.

There are times when contributions outside the ring are immeasurable. A boxing fixture in Norwich, Hugh Devlin Jr. was one of those guys with whom you wanted to have a beer, or perhaps a "Love Salad" (a trademark dish) and talk sports. The great thing about it was that you could. Devlin owned Hughie's Restaurant over on Howard Street in New London. A neighborhood restaurant, folks loved watching sports there. It even had menus shaped like boxing gloves, and memorabilia lined the walls,

Journalist and historian Sam Cohen (*right*) is pictured with elite boxer Louis "Kid" Kaplan (*left*). *Photograph courtesy of Rick Kaletsky.*

including those of his father, Hugh Devlin Sr. The elder Devlin, a talented featherweight, began his professional career in 1927. Fighting out of New Bedford, he battled against the likes of Boston's Harry Goldstein, Brooklyn's Pete DeGrasse, Brighton's Johnny Vacca and New York's Sammy Gelbar before hanging up the gloves in 1932.

There was an era when the first thing most sports enthusiasts did in the morning was grab their copy of the *Hartford Courant* and head right for Bill Lee's column, "With Malice Toward None." From the clubhouse to the doghouse, the talented sports editor always sought the truth and typically found it. Nobody, or so it seemed in those challenging times for the sport, supported the sweet science as much as Lee. And if you were a friend of his, you were for life.

Born in New London, Arthur B. McGinley finally found solace in West Hartford. His nearly seven-decade career as a newspaperman started in New London before he headed off to Providence, New York and Boston.

Following a stint in the army, during World War I, he worked for both the *Courant* and the (Hartford) *Post* before taking a job at the *Times* in 1920. As sports editor for the *Times*, and even as a raconteur, his tales became legendary. A close boyhood friend of playwright Eugene O'Neill—the dramatist based his comedy *Ah, Wilderness!* on the McGinley family—Arthur often found himself speaking for hours about the Nobel laureate.

Morally sound, Dan Parker was a crusader against corruption in boxing. There is no better example of this than his investigative journalism regarding the crooked International Boxing Club (IBC), which in the 1950s dominated boxing promotion while doing its best to ruin everything good about the fight game. Parker was born in Waterbury in 1893. After graduating from high school, he worked first as a reporter, then as city editor and sportswriter at the *Waterbury American*. In 1924, two years after joining the *Daily Mirror*, he had his own column. As a boxing writer, he was a body puncher—he saved the jabs for the beats. He also wrote for *The Ring*, the *Saturday Evening Post* and *Sport*, among other publications.

Roland A. Roy was raised in East Hartford and lived most of his life in Glastonbury, where he was a foundation contractor for forty-five years as the owner of Glastonbury Concrete and Construction. Kind, quiet and strikingly handsome, he spent his adult life volunteering for United States Amateur Boxing (USA Boxing). It was Roy's passion. Sharing his love for the sweet science became easier when he opened the popular Glastonbury restaurant Gordie's Place with Gordie Howe in 1980. Lord knows how many people dropped by the place, only to share a tale or two with Roland Roy.

From covering boxing and other sports for *Sports Illustrated* to working as president of boxing telecasts for CBS, Mort Sharnik witnessed the sport firsthand. The longtime Norwalk resident also had a propensity to be at the right place at the right time. When George Foreman reinvented himself in the 1990s, Sharnik, acting as the fighter's publicist, was there to advise the elite fighter. And he was there to assist Marlon Starling and Sean Malone Jr.

In the early 1930s, Robert Lee "Bob" Steele, along with Ed Begley, the Hartford native and Academy Award winner, entertained listeners with their radio dramas on WTIC. With the advent of television, the handsome and charismatic Steele was another who found himself at the right place at the right time. Few realize that as a youth he did a bit of boxing—he claimed to have had fifty-two amateur and eighteen professional bouts—and was always an advocate of the sweet science. Steele, along with Keyes Perrin, called the first fight broadcast over W53H FM. It was Willie Pep's impressive victory over Abe Kaufman at Foot Guard Hall on January 27, 1942.

In 1995, Joe Tessitore became familiar with Connecticut residents thanks to his work at WFSB in Hartford. Taking over the primary sports anchor role in 1997, many felt the young broadcaster was destined for bigger and better things. They were right. In 2002, Tessitore began calling boxing on ESPN as part of *Tuesday Night Fights* and *Friday Night Fights*. By 2018, he found himself doing play-by-play on *Monday Night Football*.

Instrumental to the boxing coverage of ABC Sports for over twenty years, as well as producing the boxing coverage for NBC Sports at the 1996 and 2000 Olympics, Bob Yalen has had a storied business career. Beneath it all was his profound love of the sweet science. As a former associate editor of *Ring Record Book* and *FightFax Record Book*, Yalen has an ardent knowledge of the sport, no better exemplified than his work for the International Boxing Research Organization (IBRO).

Let us also not forget the contributions of the following persons: photographer Mark Brett; *Journal Inquirer* sportswriter Sherman Cain; author Jack Cavanaugh; timekeeper and former welterweight Lou Dell; photographer Rich Esposito; Bristol ring announcer John Fitzpatrick; lieutenant governor and ring announcer Attilio "Pop" Frassinelli of Stafford Springs; photographer Emily Harney; president of the Connecticut Boxing Guild, Walter E. Johnson of East Hartford; *Hartford Courant* sports editor Albert "Bert" Keane of Montville/Hartford; popular after dinner speaker Father Robert G. Keating, a former World War II combat Chaplin and a Chaplin at the Meriden school for boys and Cheshire Reformatory; Foot Guard Hall announcer Frank Murphy; newspaper columnist Jim Murray; *Courant* wordsmith Tom Puleo; Alex and John Rinaldi of the *USA Boxing News*; Waterbury-born boxer, U.S. district judge John Joseph Sirica, who became famous for his Watergate role; and author and historian Roger Zotti.

Chapter Twelve

CASINO BOXING

I used to wonder what would happen if I fought my twin. Now I know.
—Arturo Gatti, following his first battle against Micky Ward

There is nothing comparable to the magical ambiance created by casino boxing. Nothing. Granted, our grandparents may have had Madison Square Garden on a Friday night, back in the days when you had to "Look sharp! Feel sharp! Be Sharp! With Gillette razor blades." But the razor dulled, and the lights faded on the west side of Eighth Avenue, between Forty-Ninth and Fiftieth Streets in Manhattan.

On July 9, 1975, this era officially threw up the sponge: In an attempt to emulate what once was, Madison Square Garden—acting as matchmaker and promoter—announced that it was bringing back Friday night boxing, at least for a seven-week summer trail. However, it would *not* take place in the hallowed hall of Madison Square Garden IV, but in three other locations: the Convention Center in Atlantic City, the Tropicana Hotel in Las Vegas and the Cow Palace in San Francisco. The times had changed.

The announcement wasn't a surprise. Casino boxing simply didn't happen overnight; everyone who followed the sport saw it coming. Everyone. Industry analysts, those who conducted market research studies, had predicted the transition. (By the way, they were some of the same research firms who envisioned the advent of digital photography.) When the money flowed, or the "churn and drop," be it in Nevada, New Jersey or Connecticut, confirmed the strength of professional boxing as a form of entertainment, the sweet science could start unpacking. It found a new home.

Casinos offered inimitable benefits, such as guaranteed ticket sales, free hotel rooms and even a staff at the team's disposal. Boxers loved the "vibe," and the casinos enjoyed the revenue.

Participating in all the excitement were two Connecticut venues already charting a course for boxing history: Foxwoods Resort and Casino in Mashantucket and Mohegan Sun Casino & Resort in Uncasville. Although it doesn't seem fair that the state has two outstanding options for fight fans, we sure are grateful.

FOXWOODS BOXING

Popular Rhode Island fighter Vinny Paz (Vincenzo Pazienza) held multiple titles, including the IBF lightweight and WBA light middleweight championships.

On Thursday, April 23, 1992, Foxwoods Resort in Mashantucket formally began what would be an impressive boxing chronicle. The venue, along with the team at Top Rank, converted a High Stakes Bingo & Casino into a colorful boxing forum. The sellout crowd of 2,200 fight fans, along with an ESPN national television audience, watched intently as popular heavyweight contender Tommy Morrison (31-1) knocked out Kimmuel Odum (13-9) at the 1:54 mark of the third round. Among the ringside celebrities were University of Connecticut basketball coach Jim Calhoun, WBA junior middleweight champion Vinnie Pazienza and former elite featherweight Willie Pep. Morrison was the feature attraction of a six-bout card that contained many familiar New England fighters, including Ray Oliviera.

TOP TWENTY-FIVE BOXING MATCHES IN FOXWOODS HISTORY (1992–PRESENT)

With so many great bouts to choose from, it's difficult to pick the top twenty-five matches in Foxwoods history. Nevertheless, here we go. (The fights are listed chronologically, and fighter records, which appear in parentheses, are given prior to the battle.)

NOT SINCE MARLON STARLING successfully defended his WBC welter crown in 1989 at the Civic Center in Hartford had such a large audience been drawn to a boxing event. It happened on November 8, 1994, inside the new Foxwoods Arena (it had opened in May). The draw: super middleweight Vinny "Pazmanian Devil" Pazienza. A crowd favorite, the Cranston, Rhode Island gladiator was under contract to the casino. But charisma only wins the attention of boxing fans if a fighter backs it up with performance. Regrettably, Paz, who defeated Rafael Williams, looked lethargic and drew more boos than autograph requests at the end of his fight. Both boxers scaled at 168 pounds. Fortunately, the co-feature, which saw an undefeated and impressive Rodney Toney (18-0-2) capture a challenging ten-round split decision over Charles Brewer (23-4-0), saved the evening.

It was a simply fabulous night of championship boxing: Five WBC titleholders retained their designations during a pay-per-view card inside the Arena. The highlight was Hector Acero Sanchez (32-2-2) somehow managing to draw Daniel Zaragoza over twelve rounds on June 2, 1995. Zaragoza, who scored the only knockdown and dominated the bout, looked tremendous. The fight was for the WBC world super bantamweight title. On hand were Marco Antonio Barrera, who fought on the card, and left-jab legend Larry Holmes.

A sold-out crowd (4,500) on August 7, 1997, watched as the formidable Roy Jones Jr. (175 pounds) regained the WBC light heavyweight title with an opening-round knockout of Montel Griffin (174 pounds). The expeditious end came at 2:31 into the fight. Having hit the canvas in the opening minute, Griffin was dropped by a robust left hook. Billed as "Unfinished Business," Griffin was a 4-1 underdog. For less than three minutes' worth of engagement, both fighters pocketed $1.5 million.[92]

Some believe it was the finest evening of boxing in Foxwoods history. On October 17, 1997, the resort hosted a fabulous lineup: Pernell Whitaker struggled to take a unanimous-decision victory over little-known Russian Andrey Pestryaev (Andrei Pestriaev), and WBA welter champion Ike Quartey (146 pounds) managed to battle his way back to win a majority decision over Jose Luis Lopez (147 pounds). Whitaker, who when not praising himself rarely praises others, even complimented his antagonist's determination. Pestryaev was unrelenting. Quartey, recovering from the flu, was floored in the eleventh round from a solid punch. Noting his illness, his corner begged him to scrap the contest. Yet, throughout the fight, the Ghana welterweight fought impressively behind a prolific left jab. (Later, the fight was ruled a draw due to a scoring error.)

Whenever elite fighter Roy Jones Jr. (37-1-0) entered a boxing ring to engage in combat, he would be the first to tell you that it was going to be an event, and the WBC and WBA world lightweight champion was usually correct. On November 14, 1998, Jones (171 pounds) picked up a tenth-round TKO victory over veteran Otis Grant (172 pounds). Undefeated in his previous ten fights, Grant (31-1-1) was floored in the sixth round by a right uppercut and for the final time in the tenth—the third official knockdown. Referee Arthur Mercante, noting the surrender by Grant's corner, waved off the fight at the 1:18 mark. Punch accuracy was clearly the nemesis of Grant, who, if he saw a punch angle, couldn't hit it.[93]

On August 14, 1999, southpaw Stevie Johnston (21-1-0), WBC lightweight champion, took a twelve-round unanimous decision over Angel Manfredy (28-3-1). The latter, a fan favorite and favored in the contest, was trying hard to get back into the division mix following a heartbreaking loss to Floyd Mayweather Jr. Both fighters scaled at 135 pounds. With a prolific amateur career under his belt, Johnston was nothing short of spectacular in the ring. Even in a borrowed pair of shoes, he was expected to go the distance—something he had done in his previous championship fights. And he did precisely that. Dancing around the ring with that fabulous left hand of his cocked and ready, he was the aggressor for most of the battle. The flatfooted Manfredy, who wobbled at the end of the second, was content to counter probably a bit longer than he should have been. To the credit of both fighters, when pushed to engage toe-to-toe, they conducted a punch clinic; moreover, the incredible body assaults were the highlight of the well-matched contest. In the co-feature, Arturo Gatti knocked out Reyes Munoz in the first round. Reyes, completely disoriented following "Thunder" Gatti's opening manifesto, was counted out after the bell. Later, he departed the ring on a stretcher and was taken to a nearby hospital.

Dana Rosenblatt (35-1-0), who was knocked out by Vinny Pazienza (46-7-0) in August 1996, avenged the only loss of his career with a brilliant display of boxing on November 5, 1999. Taking a twelve-round split decision against the popular Rhode Island fighter, not to mention the IBO super middleweight title, Rosenblatt, who was even floored in the third round, counter-punched to perfection. As a southpaw, he was successful at keeping Pazienza off-balance before unloading with his left. It was a close fight and extremely difficult to score. Both fighters tipped at 166 pounds.

Three monster blows—a left hook followed by two rights—to the countenance of Augie Sanchez (26-1) discharged by "Prince" Naseem Hamed (34-0) in the fourth round put an end to their bout on August 19,

2000. The TKO came at the 2:34 mark of the session and resulted in Sanchez being removed by stretcher from the ring and transported to a nearby hospital. Ironically, it was Hamed who looked in trouble early in the second round, as a knockdown was ruled a slip; the fighter nearly went down at the gong. This was Hamed's fifteenth defense of the WBO featherweight title, and an impressive one at that. Both fighters scaled at 126 pounds.

It was a punch festival! In an incredible display of punching prowess, Ben Tackie (22-2) defeated Ray "Sucra" Oliveira (42-7-1) over twelve rounds of intense boxing on August 10, 2001. According to sources who track fight statistics, the bout ranked among the most prolific punching battles ever. For Oliveira, beloved by New England fight fans, it served as merely another disappointment in a long list that he has endured over his impressive—even if he doesn't always think so—career. This was his first defense of the NABF light welterweight title. Hats off to Tackie, a native of Ghana, who nearly matched his opponent punch for punch. In the fifth round, one that hopefully won't slip between the cracks of boxing history, both fighters fought hammer and tongs for the final minute. It was good, old-fashioned brawling at its finest. All hail promoter Jimmy Burchfield for delivering an outstanding product.

When the big boys come to town, everybody wants a ticket. And why not? It was the rubber match of a solid rivalry. Evander Holyfield (37-5-1) won the first fight, while John Ruiz (37-4) took the second. And, when it was over, the uncertainty of ring superiority remained. Ruiz (232 pounds) drew Holyfield (219 pounds) over twelve momentum-shifting rounds on December 15, 2001. For Ruiz, it was his third time battling at Foxwoods; for Holyfield, it was his first. The fight marked Ruiz's first defense of his World Boxing Association heavyweight title. Meanwhile, holding both the WBC and IBF versions of the heavyweight title was Lennox Lewis. Was it exciting? Obviously. The celebrity watching alone assured that.

In another Connecticut classic, James Toney (65-4-2, 190 pounds), in an incredible upset, took a twelve-round unanimous decision over the undefeated Vassiliy Jirov (31-0, 188 pounds) on April 26, 2003. The latter was trying valiantly to defend the IBF cruiserweight title for the seventh time. The pièce de résistance of this sensational confrontation was the infighting, characterized by unrelenting counterpunching. Jirov, penalized one point for a low blow in the eighth, hit the canvas in the twelfth round. Toney's margin of victory, ever so slight, was enough to grab him a title. The impressive contest was recognized by many as the 2003 "Fight of the Year." Also on the card, Antonio Tarver captured the vacant IBF and

Left: The professional achievements of elite boxer Evander "The Real Deal" Holyfield could fill this book. In 1996, the WBA presented the boxer with the Muhammad Ali Award for becoming a three-time heavyweight champion.

Right: Prolific Michigan-born fighter James "Lights Out" Toney held multiple titles, including the IBF middleweight, IBF super middleweight and IBF cruiserweight championships.

WBC light heavyweight titles in a unanimous twelve-round decision over Montell Griffin. Both fighters tipped at 175 pounds. Tarver, in a command performance, won every round on all three scorecards. Down in both the first and last rounds, Griffin nearly had both eyes swollen shut by the end of the engagement. The titles had been vacated when Roy Jones Jr. opted for a heavyweight crusade.

In a thrilling night not only for Brazilian boxing fans but also for all of boxing, Acelino Freitas (135 pounds) seized victory over the undefeated Artur Grigorian (36-0) in a twelve-round unanimous decision. The match, held on January 3, 2004, was particularly eventful, as it was Grigorian's eighteenth defense of his WBO lightweight title. A stunned crowd of 1,400 watched as an undeniable Freitas (34-0) dropped his adversary four times during the upset. For Freitas, who already held the WBO and WBA junior lightweight titles, it was another belt for his trophy case.[94]

In a fascinating bout, Diego Corrales (37-2), who was leveled in the tenth round, defeated Joel Casamayor (30-1) in a twelve-round split decision on March 6, 2004. Both boxers scaled at 130 pounds. With the victory, Corrales picked up the vacant World Boxing Organization junior lightweight title (vacated by Acelino Freitas) and the IBA super featherweight title. Casamayor had defeated Corrales when they met in October 2003. Corrales, having employed the assistance of Casamayor's former trainer, Joe Goosen, made the battle a chess match. Goosen kept his mobile fighter calm while instructing him to fight behind the jab. Casamayor, the 1992 Olympic gold medal winner for Cuba, had a new trainer, Buddy McGirt. No introduction was needed for the elite fighting skills of McGirt. However, why his fighter was relatively inactive for the first six rounds remains a mystery. It was an extraordinarily close yet entertaining crusade.

Speaking of Corrales (38-2), on August 7, 2004, he garnered a tenth-round TKO over the undefeated Acelino Freitas (35-0) in a WBO lightweight title bout. It was a shocking surrender, as champion Freitas, bruised, battered and decked three times, arose from his final knockdown only to inform referee Mike Ortega that he did not want to continue. The submission came at the 1:24 mark of the tenth term and was witnessed by a sellout crowd of a bit over three thousand people. The contest was fought at a brisk pace, and Corrales (135 pounds) inflicted considerable damage with his solid right hand. Resorting to stalling tactics, an exhausted Freitas (134 pounds) was penalized one point in the ninth for repeatedly spitting out his mouthpiece.

In a valiant display, New England super middle Scott Pemberton (26-3-1) defeated Omar Sheika (23-5) via a tenth-round TKO on January 23, 2004. The conflict was simply a merciless display conducted by two talented young gladiators, and the sellout crowd was mesmerized. Both fighters hit the canvas, with Pemberton down in rounds two and six. For Sheika, dropped with two minutes remaining in the tenth, it was his first career visit to the canvas. Although he was able to find his feet, it was a prelude to the inevitable: Pemberton unloaded on Sheika and forced referee Gary Rosato to stop the fight at the 1:43 mark of the tenth. For Pemberton, a fan favorite, it was his first successful defense of the NABF super middle title and his second of the IBU super middle crown. Both fighters scaled at 168 pounds.

Acelino "Popo" Freitas, considered a celebrity in Brazil, gradually developed an impressive New England fan base. And, being as skillful of a lightweight as he was, it was no surprise. Although he briefly fought after 2007, his last two North American appearances took place at Foxwoods.

The first came on April 29, 2006, when he took an action-filled twelve-round split decision over Zahir Raheem (27-1) for the vacant WBO world lightweight title. Both participants scaled at 135 pounds. The first three rounds were a free-for-all, but by the seventh, it had settled down to solid boxing. While Freitas (37-1) took command, Raheem landed some of the bigger shots during the intensely close contest. Announcing his retirement as a professional boxer on October 4, 2006, Freitas, like many fighters, had second thoughts. Later, the WBO reinstated him as its lightweight champion.

On April 28, 2007, Freitas (38-1) returned to Foxwoods for another memorable engagement: the one-hundredth professional boxing card at the venue. But the evening wouldn't end the way the fighter had hoped. Taking on undefeated Juan Diaz (31-0), the WBA light champion, proved to be an overwhelming challenge. Noting the damage incurred by his fighter at the conclusion of the eighth round, Freitas's trainer, Oscar Suarez, stopped the fight. The more than three thousand fight fans in attendance were disappointed, but it was a prudent action. Both boxers scaled at 135 pounds.

In a prolific punching battle on March 7, 2008, veteran Cristobal Cruz (126 pounds) seized a twelve-round majority decision over an impressive Thomas Mashaba (125 pounds). However, it was a close contest. The relatively unknown Mashaba (20-1-4) entered the battle with a ten-fight winning streak. This was the South African's first contest in the United States. Cruz (35-11-1), who hailed from Tijuana, Mexico, fought in his aggressive trademark style that nearly had Mashaba blinded by the end of the contest.

On April 25, 2009, undefeated Carl Froch (167 pounds), the newly crowned WBC super middleweight champion, managed to defeat Jermain Taylor (166 pounds), a determined and former undisputed middleweight champion, with just 0:29 remaining in the final round. Having staggered Taylor (28-2-1) early in round twelve, Froch (24-0) offloaded a tremendous volley of punches, most unanswered, that dropped his rival. Referee Mike Ortega, watching Taylor struggle to rise at the count of nine, had little choice but to stop the fight. To Taylor's credit, Froch was knocked down late in the third round for the first time in his career.

London's Andy Lee (24-1) captured a tenth-round TKO over Scotland's undefeated Craig McEwan (19-0). The fight, with all its UK underpinnings, took place on March 12, 2011. It was a momentum-shifting battle since nearly the beginning of the bout. Lee sent McEwan to the canvas in the ninth round. Unable to clear the cobwebs, McEwan still came out for the tenth round. It was a bad idea. Struck by a crushing left to the jaw by his waiting rival, McEwan fell face-first to the canvas. The fight was stopped at the 0:56 mark of the final round. It was undeniably a dreamland punch, and referee Steve Smoger bypassed a count. Both fighters scaled at 162 pounds. For the dominant southpaw Lee, it was his last ring visit to Connecticut.

The Fight, Ortiz v. Berto I

The battle between Victor Ortiz (28-2-2) and Andre Berto (27-0) for the WBC welterweight championship on April 16, 2011, had all the makings of a classic contest. On paper, it certainly appeared that way. But fight media hyperbole, as everyone understood, had to be taken with a grain of salt. Granted, Berto was the third-ranked welterweight by *The Ring* magazine, and Ortiz failed to even be recognized by the publication. But Ortiz, a 3-1 betting underdog, hadn't lost a fight since June 2009. Regardless, most fight fans believed Berto was bound for stardom and that this was his launching pad. Well, to put it mildly, the launch was scrubbed.

Victor Ortiz virtually dominated his rival and scored a unanimous twelve-round decision victory. It took only a couple of rounds for those in attendance to realize they were watching something special.

Here is a round-by-round assessment of the fight. The excitement began in the first round. Ortiz delivered a left hand that dropped Berto at the 1:49 mark; it was not ruled a knockdown. Berto then caught a straight right hand that sent him backward and into a corner at the 1:11 mark. Ortiz then unloaded the chamber until Berto's left knee hit the canvas. The crowd was on its feet for the final minute of the round. Although it was clear that Berto was struggling in the second round, a clean right hand caught Ortiz and nearly sent him down with thirty seconds remaining; it was ruled an official knockdown. As the momentum shifted in the third, Ortiz looked more determined than ever to take the fight. He was quick, aggressive and far more prolific than Berto. Looking a bit tired, Berto clinched often, especially when his back was against the ropes. Meanwhile, Ortiz utilized his right uppercut to perfection. Berto, clearly confused by the offensive assault of his rival, failed to implement a counter strategy. Appearing tired, he was backing into the ropes simply hoping that Ortiz would tire. Ortiz, working behind an impressive left hand, continued to dominate in round four. He proceeded with his almost systematic destruction of Berto in round five. Meanwhile, Berto, who looked out of condition, ignored his corner's instruction to start moving. The fighter was taking far too many punches, and they were concerned. Showing signs of life in the sixth term, Berto was scoring with his short right punches. Then, with a minute left in the round, he dropped Ortiz with a fabulous right hand. Seeing that turnabout was fair play, Ortiz leveled Berto with only six seconds remaining in the round. Pulling back a bit from his offensive assaults, Ortiz decided to merely box. Withstanding a couple of nice shots from Berto, he continued to impress

In a unanimous-decision victory, Victor Ortiz defeated Andre Berto over twelve rounds. For the latter, it was his sixth WBC welterweight title defense. *Emily Harney / Fightography* ©.

in round seven. Once again, the momentum shifted as Berto, on his toes, delivered a skillful performance in round eight. In round nine, Ortiz looked rested—as recharged as one can be in a slugfest of this nature. Berto, who had been off the ropes for a couple of rounds, was trying to stay in the middle of the ring. Warned the previous round for hitting Berto behind the head, Ortiz failed to listen and had a point deducted in round ten. Referee Ortega, who was conspicuous the entire bout, continued to maintain control of the fight—perhaps too much so, according to some. Ortiz, dominating with uppercuts, had Berto, who appeared exhausted, back on the ropes in the eleventh round. The final round began with Berto flexing some muscle with two solid shots—a right and a left—in the first minute. However, Ortiz took the reins the rest of the way.

For his efforts, Ortiz won the fight (his first as a welter) and the WBC welter crown. And he handed his adversary his first loss. Berto left the launching pad wondering what had happened. By the way, he wasn't alone. Replacing him in the rocket to stardom, or so it appeared, was southpaw Victor Ortiz,

Leading up to the contest, Victor Ortiz hadn't lost a contest since June 2009, and Berto was undefeated. *Emily Harney / Fightography ©.*

hailing from Ventura, California. However, this rocket also failed to take off; Ortiz lost his next three consecutive battles against the likes of Floyd Mayweather Jr., Josesito Lopez and Luis Collazo. He would battle Berto again, in 2016, only to get knocked out in the fourth round.

Vanes "The Nightmare" Martirosyan (34-1-1) defeated Willie "The Great" Nelson by way of a ten-round unanimous decision on October 4, 2014. Both boxers tipped at 153 pounds. With the victory, Martirosyan, a 2004 U.S. Olympian, retained the WBO Inter-Continental light middleweight title. For the lanky Nelson, with a reach advantage of nearly five inches, it was a disappointing loss. He had been victorious in his previous two battles at Foxwoods. Nelson took command early with that outstanding right hand of his and wisely did so at a distance. And distance was the key to victory, as Martirosyan fully intended, and did, bring the fight to Nelson. Martirosyan, a quicker puncher, also did an excellent job of counter-punching; specifically, going over Nelson's jab with his accurate overhand rights.

There are times in boxing when you have to enter the ring and make a statement with your performance. For undefeated Jermall Charlo (21-0), that time came on September 12, 2015, when he defeated Cornelius Bundrage (34-5-0), the IBF world super welterweight champion, by way of a third-round TKO. Both boxers tipped at 153 pounds. Bundrage, down in rounds one and two and twice in round three, ended up being a perfect target for Charlo's overhand right, left jab, left hook and straight right hand.

On April 16, 2016, undefeated Joe Pedraza (21-0) took a twelve-round unanimous decision over Stephen Smith (23-1). Both fighters scaled at 129 pounds. It was a fairly even match entering the ninth round. That's when Pedraza dropped Smith with a fierce right hand to the chin. Pedraza, who appeared to be executing a battle plan, was a far more accurate puncher. The desperation, which gradually intensified on the face of Smith, became evident after the ninth session. The battle was for the IBF world super feather crown.

Middleweight Sergiy Derevanchenko (8-0) defeated former world titleholder Sam Soliman (44-13) with an impressive second-round TKO. The fight, on July 21, 2016, was stopped at the 2:41 mark.[95] Both fighters weighed in at 159 pounds. A Derevanchenko (left-right) combination to the head dropped Soliman on one knee for a six count in the first round. Then he dropped Soliman with three powerful rights and a crushing left hook in the second. When a groggy Soliman rose and the action resumed, he was dropped again. Referee Johnny Callas waived it off as Soliman was lying on his back. The contest, an IBF middleweight voluntary elimination bout, moved Derevanchenko a step closer, or so it was believed, to a mandatory shot against Gennady Golovkin. After winning four of his next five contests, Derevanchenko lost to Golovkin in 2019.

HONORABLE MENTIONS

On August 5, 1997, Reggie Green (25-2-0), the number-one contender, dominated champion Ray Oliveira (30-5-0) over twelve rounds to take a unanimous decision and the NABF super lightweight title. Oliveira, a Connecticut favorite, was nonstop during the first three rounds, only to become confused when Green switched tactics to a more fluid and moving target.

Vernon Forrest (39-2), WBC super welterweight champion, dropped opponent Michele Piccirillo (48-3) three times—in the sixth, ninth and eleventh rounds—on the way to a TKO victory at the 2:21 mark of the eleventh frame. It was Forrest's accurate overhand right that was responsible for the bulk of the damage to Piccirillo, who was one pound lighter (152 pounds) than his opponent. The fight took place on December 1, 2007.

There are two other contests worth mentioning. On October 13, 2000, on the Rosenblatt/McIntyre undercard, middleweight Kassim Ouma (10-1) took a nice six-round unanimous decision victory over undefeated Kuvonchbek Toygonbaev (12-0). And on December 2, 2000, Ray Oliveira (41-7-1) took a twelve-round majority decision over Vince Phillip (41-5-1) to capture the vacant NABF light welterweight title.

"IT'S AN ARGUMENT," BERT Randolph Sugar used to quip with regard to constructing a boxing list. Or, as he saw it, it is an unnecessary action that leaves the source helplessly against the ropes. Nevertheless, we will move on to Uncasville, Connecticut.

TOP TWENTY BOXING MATCHES IN MOHEGAN SUN HISTORY (1996–PRESENT)

Venturing into deep water again, here are the top twenty matches in Mohegan Sun history, listed chronologically. Believing in the old Faulkner adage, "You cannot swim for new horizons until you have courage to lose sight of the shore," it is time to venture into deep water.

SETTING A BRISK PACE, lightweight champion Phillip Holiday, a prolific puncher, managed a twelve-round unanimous decision over an impressive Ivan Robinson. This was the first show in the facility for HBO's popular *Boxing After Dark*. Ivan "Mighty" Robinson (134 pounds) entered the fight a year younger, three inches taller and with a reach advantage of two inches. Trained by Tommy Brooks, Robinson (23-0) understood the difficult task in front of him. In his fifth title defense (IBF lightweight championship) in thirteen months, South African Phillip Holiday (135 pounds), whose trademark was conditioning, entered the fight 29-0 with sixteen knockouts. Superb defensive movement by a svelte Holiday allowed him to duck a considerable number of Robinson's punches. Holiday's magnificent body assault slowed his rival, but not enough for Holiday to deliver his powerful overhand right. Both fighters worked at an extraordinary pace. A standing ovation at the end of this December 21, 1996 battle validated a brilliant performance.[96]

When two evenly matched pugilists collide, it typically yields abundant action.[97] Six years and three weight classes removed from their first encounter at middleweight, James "Lights Out" Toney (181 pounds, 53-3-2), battling as a cruiserweight, needed to pull the plug on Mike "The Bodysnatcher" McCallum (182 pounds, 49-4-1). And in the final chapter of their trilogy, he did so again on February 22, 1997. It was Toney's second defeat of McCallum. (They drew in their first meeting.) The twelve-round unanimous verdict, along with the vacant WBU cruiserweight championship, went to the conspicuous, yet accurate, James Toney.

An undefeated "Sugar" Shane Mosley (23-0), who was rated at the time as the best pound-for-pound boxer in the world, seized a twelve-round unanimous decision victory over undefeated IBF lightweight champion Phillip "No Deal" Holiday (31-0). Mosley did a magnificent job of shutting down the body attack of Holiday by blocking and moving. The talented South African, unable to strike with the degree of accuracy necessary to defeat the mobile Mosley, simply could not alter the tempo of the bout.[98] The fight took place on August 2, 1997, and both boxers tipped at 135 pounds.

Fast-forward 116 days. Destined to prove the critics wrong—or at least those who thought his title battle against Holiday was lackluster—Shane Mosley (135 pounds), in his first title defense (IBF lightweight), scored an eleventh-round KO over Mexican challenger Manuel Gomez (17-8) in Texas on November 25, 1997. Still, his critics weren't convinced of his "pound-for-pound" best-fighter status; consequently, his battle against Demetrio Ceballos (135 pounds) on February 6, 1998, at Mohegan Sun had to make a statement. And, true to form, Mosley (24-0) did just that. Scoring an impressive eighth-round TKO over Ceballos (20-1), "Sugar Shane" was ever so sweet. Ceballos, two years younger and two inches smaller than his antagonist, was floored in the fourth round by an overhand right and two left hooks to the body. Following a low blow by his opponent, Ceballos was stunned by a solid right before being dropped by a volley of Mosley combinations in the eighth. The champion's TKO victory officially came at the 2:34 mark of the eighth round.

The big boys were in the house. Since recapturing the WBC heavyweight title in 1997, Lennox Lewis (33-1) had made three successful defenses and even added the Lineal heavyweight title to his résumé. While he had hoped for a unification match with WBA and IBF heavyweight champion Evander Holyfield, such was not the case, so he agreed to battle the WBC's number-one contender, the undefeated Croatian fighter Željko Mavrović (27-0). Although dominating most of the fight, through control and prolific punching, Lewis (243 pounds), a slow starter, could not get his opponent (214 pounds) to give ground. Still, his performance was enough to grab the twelve-round unanimous decision victory on September 26, 1998. The battle, held in the outdoor pavilion at Mohegan Sun, drew an estimated four thousand fight fans.[99]

In a fight recalled not for its victory but for a particular action, an undefeated Zab Judah (21-0) knocked out South African Jan Piet Bergman (38-2) during their February 12, 2000 clash at "The Sun." But it was a second-round knockdown, not the fourth-round knockout, that caught everyone by surprise. Judah (138 pounds) was caught right on the point of the chin and thrust to the canvas. It was the first time he had been down in his career. Not badly hurt, the fighter popped right back up. Contributing to the intensity of the surprise was that Judah had dropped Bergman twice in the opening round. In the fourth, a hard left followed by a combination to the head of Bergman began Judah's assault that eventually leveled Bergman (139 pounds) at the 2:50 mark. The South African's attempt at a retreat had failed. With the victory, Judah captured the vacant IBF super lightweight title (Terron Millet had been stripped of the crown).

On August 5, 2000, on the undercard of the Judah/Millet feature, Juan Lazcano (135 pounds, 23-2-1) captured a controversial ten-round split-decision victory over Jesse James Leija (136 pounds, 40-4-2). Nicknamed "Hispanic Causing Panic," Mexican-born Lazcano had become a popular boxer, especially among Latinos. To fight fans in attendance, it looked as if veteran Leija had been in control for the majority of the battle, but the cards tallied differently.

When undefeated Kirk "Bubba" Johnson (233 pounds, 29-0-1) challenged PABA heavyweight champion Oleg Maskaev (230 pounds, 20-2) for his crown, the 1992 Olympian (Canada) wasn't intimidated, nor was he worried about the odds. The Russian champion was a slight favorite. Having recently come off an impressive TKO victory over Marcus Johnson, he was confident. However, as the first couple of rounds ticked off, it was evident that that optimism was fading. Maskaev was taking more and more control of the battle. Then, at the start of the third round, Johnson managed, in one of those rare moments that boxers often dream about, to catch his rival off guard with a powerful overhand right that stunned Maskaev. Locked in, Johnson followed with a huge left hook flush to his rival's chin that sent him crashing to the canvas. Rising in time for a second wave, Maskaev, pinned to the ropes, became merely a target. The knockout, on October 7, 2000, came at the 0:51 mark of round four. Maskaev, barely conscious, fell through the bottom two ropes, onto the apron and into the ringside observers.[100]

Defending his World Boxing Council and World Boxing Association super lightweight titles at Mohegan Sun on June 23, 2001, Kostya Tszyu (26-1) was sanguine as ever. And why not, as the Australian boxer hadn't experienced a loss since 1997, and that was against Vince Phillips in an enormous upset. Hoping to quickly defeat German fighter Oktay Urkal (28-0) in a mandatory defense, Tszyu (139 pounds) would next face Zab Judah in a unification matchup. Or so he hoped. First, he needed this victory, on this night. But the undefeated Urkal (138 pounds), an Olympic silver medalist, had no intention of rolling over and pacifying the champion. When Tszyu, working behind a snappy left jab that set up his trademark overhand right, managed to break Urkal's

Australian boxer Kostya "Thunder from Down Under" Tszyu held multiple titles, including the IBF light welterweight, WBC light welterweight, WBA light welterweight and IBF light welterweight championships.

jaw in the seventh round, the posture of the battle subtly shifted. Since the damage was not immediately evident, the German managed to mask the injury. Throwing a flurry of punches in the twelfth and final round, Urkal, who fought a magnificent battle, had Tszyu back on his heels twice. Although the decision for Tszyu was anticipated, the 3,300 fans in attendance couldn't resist booing the results.

The Fight, Ward versus Gatti, I

One, or perhaps two, handfuls of classic boxing matches will occur during a boxing fan's lifetime. If they are lucky. And if they are extremely lucky, they will have an opportunity to witness one of these events in person. On May 18, 2002, Micky Ward, a blue-collar journeyman from Lowell, Massachusetts, with a look of pure innocence, courageously handed Arturo Gatti, an Italian Canadian boxer who hailed from New Jersey with a countenance that looked as if he shaved blindfolded, a ten-round majority decision defeat. For the 6,254 fans in attendance, it was a bar brawl, a street fight, an old-fashioned club battle. Regardless of how it was framed, afterward, there wasn't a soul inside the arena who didn't realize they had just witnessed boxing history.

Without a belt on the line, only pride, two unassuming gladiators came to scratch unaware of what part, if any, destiny would play in their confrontation. Both were warriors, identical in nearly all factors: height, weight and reach. The only variables were age and heart.

Here is a round-by-round glimpse at history. Graceful yet dominating Gatti took the first round while guaranteeing that Ward's cut man, Al Gavin, was in for a long night. Ward was cut on the right eye. Gatti controlled most of the second while taking his first of many Ward left hooks to the body. The Jersey boy, warned for a low blow, continued to deliver punches at nearly three times the rate of his rival. Ward continued his body assault as the real slugging began in the third. Successfully targeting Gatti's optic in the fourth, Ward tried to take a frustrated Gatti out of his game but drew combination fire in return. Moments before the fourth round closed, Ward shuddered from a left south of the border. Gatti was docked a point. Ward withstood the prolific assaults of Gatti to deliver an incredible round-ending volley of fourteen unanswered punches in round five. Amazingly, Gatti took the sixth and seventh rounds. After dominating most of the eighth round, Gatti suddenly became a punching bag for the final forty-five seconds and endured a tremendous left uppercut followed by a combination that backed

"Irish" Micky Ward is often recalled for his trilogy with Arturo Gatti (2002–3). The Massachusetts fighter won the first fight, and Gatti won the next two.

him into the ropes, where Ward unloaded. The ninth round—*The Ring* magazine's 2002 Round of the Year and *USA Today*'s 2002 Round of the Year—became one for the books. Gatti was floored for nearly a full count, rose, then took a full magazine from Ward. Miraculously still standing, Gatti switched fuel tanks then unloaded on an exhausted Ward. But the tanks ran dry. The round drew to a conclusion with Gatti's trainer, Buddy McGirt, towel in hand, and referee Frank Cappuccino seconds from ending the fight. Gatti, searching for reality, somehow managed to survive. Over one hundred power punches marked perhaps the round of the century. The tenth and final round began with Ward thinking, based on the scene in Gatti's corner, that the fight

The unveiling of a stunning commemorative banner to hang inside Mohegan Sun. *The Ring* magazine named the battle between Micky Ward and Arturo Gatti, held on May 18, 2002, its Fight of the Year.

was over. It was not. Gatti, likely through divine intervention, reloaded and delivered a convincing performance. It was as if round nine had never taken place. Neither fighter had any business surviving, not after what they had endured. Yet, as both leaned on each other cheek to cheek and the final seconds tolled, they embraced, each hoping the other could hold them up. The majority decision was given to Ward. Although the cheers subdued the groans, there were no losers on this night.

The fight was the Boxing Writers Association of America Fight of the Year for 2002 and *The Ring*'s Fight of the Year for 2002. It catapulted Mohegan Sun Arena into the pantheon of great venues, alphabetically behind Madison Square Garden.

Drawing tremendous inspiration from his family, Fernando Montiel was the youngest of four brothers, all of whom boxed, three professionally.[101] This was not a surprise, considering that their father, Manuel Sr., found his passion in the ring and even fought elite boxer Miguel Canto. Undefeated,

Montiel (26-0-1) had faced challenges in his career, perhaps none as great as Mark Johnson (41-3-0). Returning to the ring in 2001, Johnson, also with his fair share of baggage, was trying desperately to reignite his career. As a former two-division champion, he sensed the urgency, even if he appeared a bit lethargic at first. When he dropped Montiel in the fifth round with a perfect right hook, the writing was on the wall.[102] Inflicting the first loss in Fernando Montiel's career via a tight twelve-round majority decision, Johnson picked up the vacant WBO junior bantamweight title and was now a three-time world champion. Both boxers conducted business on August 16, 2003, at 115 pounds.

In one of those "it looks good on paper, so you gotta go" battles, Ronald "Winky" Wright (49-3-0), ranked number one by the WBA and the WBC, seized a twelve-round unanimous decision over the prolific-punching Sam Soliman (31-7-0), who was rated number one by the IBF. It was the speedy Soliman's first loss in over four years. Wright, far from a power puncher, didn't think his Australian adversary had the endurance to keep up with him. He was wrong. Soliman's strategy was to deliver swift combinations at peculiar angles, followed by an expeditious retreat. Countering every Wright assault, he believed, would win him rounds. Although both fighters weighed in at 159 pounds, it was clear that Wright may have spent his hours after the weigh-in at Season Buffet inside Mohegan Sun, putting a little extra weight behind those southpaw punches. The crowd, some of whom had fallen in love with the energetic and prolific style of Soliman, did not agree with the verdict. The fight took place on December 10, 2005.

A 1997 National Junior Olympic amateur champion, at 119 pounds, Steven Luevano (30-1-0) had almost three hundred amateur bouts before turning professional in 2000. His opponent on July 21, 2006, in a battle for the NABO featherweight crown, was veteran Cristóbal Cruz Rivera (32-7-1).[103] Evenly matched, both fighters brought their fair share of duplicitous practices into the ring. Inevitably, referee Arthur Mercante Jr. had to remind both men of the benefits of clean punches during the first half of the battle. But in the end, it was Luevano by a twelve-round unanimous decision. Both boxers scaled at 126 pounds. Having been unfairly credited with a knockdown (the blow was south of the border) in round three, Luevano landed a crisp body shot that felled Cruz in the ninth.[104]

Paulie Malignaggi, the charismatic Brooklyn Italian with the million-dollar smile, posted twenty-one consecutive victories before suffering his first loss. It came via a unanimous decision to Miguel Cotto on June 10, 2006, at Madison Square Garden. Despite being pounded into a bloody mess and suffering a broken right cheekbone, Malignaggi would not relent. Over a year later, on June 16, 2007, Malignaggi, now sporting golden locks, faced Lovemore Ndou (45-8-1), the scrappy Australian welterweight. It was one of those evenings in which referee Eddie Cotton delivered more warnings than a lighthouse on a foggy night. Ndou was warned in the third for kidney punches during a clinch and in the fifth, sixth (point deducted) and eleventh for rabbit punching.[105] Hoping to throw Malignaggi (22-1-0) off his game, Ndou switched to southpaw during the seventh. It didn't work. Spotting an opening in the ninth round, Malignaggi tumbled Ndou with an abrupt right hand. To no surprise, the unanimous twelve-round decision was awarded to Paulie Malignaggi. Both fighters weighed in at 138 pounds.

When Andy Lee (15-0), with that solid southpaw left of his, floored Brian Vera (15-1) in the first round of their scheduled ten-round middleweight contest, many felt it was going to be an abbreviated main event. Then, when Lee (158 3/4 pounds) dominated most of the first five rounds of the affair, everyone was certain of it. And they were right, but not for the reasons they thought. Austin's Brian Vera (162 pounds) upset Ireland's Andy Lee in a surprise turnabout of events. Vera merely stayed the course and maintained his brawling approach, and it worked. He had been warned for holding and hitting, and also for hitting off the break.[106] Lee, who absorbed a considerable amount of damage in the sixth round—his knees buckled more than once— simply could not absorb the beating he was given by Vera in the seventh. Referee Tony Chiarantano, with little choice, stopped the contest with forty-three seconds left in the seventh round. It was the right call. As a result, Lee was handed his first career loss on March 21, 2008.

When they first met, Carlos Quintana simply dominated Paul Williams over twelve rounds. But that was then, and this was now. In a stunning upset, Williams (33-1), slightly ahead in the odds, delivered Quintana (25-1) by way of a technical knockout at the 2:15 mark of the opening round. Both fighters weighed in at 146 pounds for their contest on June 7, 2008. Incidentally, Williams was five years younger, was taller and had a greater reach. Quintana, a southpaw, was defending his World Boxing Organization welterweight title for the first time. At about the 1:30 mark of the first, the fireworks began. Williams landed a combination, forcing his rival headfirst into a clinch. Quintana managed to push Williams into the ropes, and both fought out of a break. Sensing the damage, Williams fired combinations until a final left hook delivered his antagonist to the canvas. Answering referee Eddie Claudio's eight count, Quintana shook his head in affirmation that he was fine. Williams then caught his adversary with a left that sent him into the ropes. Quintana managed to fight out as far as the center of the ring before Williams's relentless combinations eventually backed him into an opposite corner. Claudio, sensing the fighter's condition, waved it off prior to both fighters falling to the floor.

Danbury's Delvin Rodriguez, the IBF's number-two contender, fought Isaac Hlatshwayo to draw in their fight in November 2008, in the latter's home country of South Africa. It was a draw, despite Rodriguez sending his antagonist to the canvas in the ninth round. Hell-bent to avenge the injustice, Rodriguez (24-2-2) entered the Mohegan Sun ring on August 1, 2009, to face his welterweight rival (28-1-1) for the vacant International Boxing Federation crown. Rodriguez, two years younger and three inches taller than his opponent, tipped at 147 pounds, or a pound heavier than Hlatshwayo. Taking command early, Hlatshwayo, gloves held high, worked behind his impressive left jab. Rodriguez, having difficulty penetrating the defense of his rival, fell into more of a counter-strategy as the fight wore on. Unfortunately for the Ulster County–trained fighter, he fell a few points short and lost the twelve-round split decision.

Ranked southpaw welterweight Devon Alexander (139 pounds), aka "Alexander the Great," lived up to his moniker by disposing of Juan Urango (140 pounds) by way of a TKO at the 1:12 mark of the eighth round. Alexander (19-0), a former amateur star who won multiple national titles as a teenager, relied on his technical skills to carry him, and they did. A knockout artist who packed a punch, Urango (22-2-1) was looking for his perfect shot but never found it. In the eighth round, Alexander struck Urango with a vicious uppercut that launched the fighter to his back. Returning to the deck, Urango was game. Seconds later, Alexander, with a solid right, dropped his antagonist for the final time. Sensing the damage, referee Benjy Esteves Jr. waved it off. Urango was stopped for the first time in his career. For his victory, Alexander, who already held the WBC world super lightweight title, added the IBF version. The scheduled twelve-round battle took place on March 6, 2010.

Aware of who he was facing, Sergey Kovalev (19-0-1) dropped Gabriel Campillo (21-4-1), the former WBA light heavyweight champion, with a robust left hook in the third round. The technical knockout came at the 1:30 mark. Known for being a slow starter, Campillo should have anticipated the vigorous attack by his adversary and acted accordingly. His failure cost him the fight. From the opening bell, Kovalev fired volley after volley of combinations at his lethargic target. Hurt early in the third, Campillo hit the canvas three times before the bout concluded. The contest took place on January 19, 2013, and both fighters tipped at 175 pounds. Kovalev, who knocked out 85 percent of the fighters he faced, continued his pace to become a major factor in the division. As for Campillo, a polished and accurate southpaw, his book needed to be rewritten to include a powerful opening.

It was WBC International and WBC Continental Americas cruiserweight champion Constantin Bejenaru (12-0) of Brooklyn, New York, defending his titles against number-one-ranked mandatory contender Thabiso Mchunu (18-3) of Kato Ridge, South Africa, in a ten-round main event on November 25, 2017. Most felt Bejenaru had the fight in his pocket and that it was only a matter of time. In round seven, when Bejenaru dropped Mchunu with a precision left cross, many felt the end was near. But Bejenaru couldn't capitalize on his opportunity, and Mchunu, to his credit, went the distance. In the end, it was the champion in a ten-round unanimous decision. Both fighters scaled at two hundred pounds.

HONORABLE MENTIONS

With so many great battles at "The Sun," it was even harder to select the honorable mentions. But here are three to digest.

CHRIS BYRD (211½ POUNDS, 36-2), defending his IBF heavyweight title for the first time, did so successfully by taking a twelve-round unanimous decision over a somewhat shocked Fres Oquendo (224 pounds, 24-1-0). But not everyone in the audience on September 20, 2003, agreed with the verdict. Similar to a bottle of New England maple syrup being poured over breakfast pancakes, the fight started out slow but picked up—by the sixth round, to be specific. Fresh off an impressive unanimous-decision victory over Evander Holyfield, Byrd exhibited less speed and style than in his previous battle. Failing to find a rhythm, he stumbled three times to the canvas, but none were ruled knockdowns. As the battle progressed, Byrd knew it was close and understood that he was rolling the dice on a decision. Back to the pancake analogy: even the *HBO World Championship Boxing* team calling the fight had trouble swallowing the verdict. It must be the syrup.

Oh, the sweet pain of anticipation, a feeling known to every boxing fan. When veteran "Fast" Eddie Chambers (196 pounds) decided to move down to cruiserweight and make his division debut at Mohegan Sun on August 3, 2013, fight fans were ecstatic. Chambers (33-3), having disappointed in his recent heavyweight appearances, was scheduled for ten rounds against an unknown Thabiso Mchunu (13-1). Seemingly baffled by the southpaw counter-punching of the South African, the thirty-one-year-old Chambers offered little more than a pitiful performance. Ironically, with the ten-round unanimous decision victory, it was Mchunu (199 pounds) who emerged as a new contender, not Chambers. Although the crowd was unimpressed by the lack of early engagement in the battle, most, following an outpouring of booing, felt they may have seen something special.

If you were sitting among the two thousand fans at the Uncas Pavilion on May 19, 2001, and watching the first two and one-third rounds of the battle between Antwun Echols (165 pounds) and Charlie Brewer (167 pounds), you probably believed you were witnessing one of the finest battles in years. Down three times in the second round, Echols (24-4-1) somehow managed to stop Brewer (36-7) at 1:21 in the third and win the North American Boxing Association super middleweight title. Brewer, who took a standing eight count but continued, was rocked again before referee Michael Ortega stepped in and waved it off.[107] The crowd, livid over the action, couldn't understand why each time Echols was leveled he was given an eight count and allowed to continue, while Brewer wasn't allowed such luxury. Afterward, Ortega confirmed that the fighter could not protect himself and thus action was needed.

WHILE IT MAY BE difficult to believe that time has gone by so quickly, these forty-five ring battles are a testament to the excitement and quality of casino boxing. Both Foxwoods Resort and Casino in Mashantucket and Mohegan Sun Casino & Resort in Uncasville have not only added to the rich history of Connecticut boxing, but they have also taken it to an entirely new level. I'll say it for you: "Thank you."

So, with all of these great past performances, you may be asking yourself, What's next for professional boxing? Although nobody can be certain, there are some signs. Floyd Mayweather's 2013 pact with Showtime covered six fights and thirty months. Although the value was never publicly released, the deal guaranteed Mayweather roughly a minimum of $200 million. In addition to media agreements, headlining residency seems to be the logical next step. Yep, although professional boxers are not musical acts, they are entertainment. The productions will be far more elaborate, with everything from exhibits about the fighter's life to several weeks of special events. Imagine taking a trip through boxing history with the current champion. Imagine watching him or her as they spend weeks in training, attending special "meet and greet" sessions, listening to lectures about the fight game or even playing a round of golf with the champion. I, for one, can't wait.

Chapter Thirteen

CONNECTICUT BOXING HALL OF FAME

Mediocrity knows nothing higher than itself; but talent instantly recognizes genius.
—Arthur Conan Doyle, The Valley of Fear

In 1662, three colonies—Connecticut, Saybrook and New Haven—were merged under a royal charter that made Connecticut a Crown colony. As the southernmost state in the New England region of what is now the northeastern United States and one of the thirteen colonies that rejected British rule, it surprises few that an independent frame of mind, not to mention a willingness to defend it, seems inherent in the Connecticut mindset. Since the days when British troops landed along the state's coastline, pugilism has been a form of both entertainment and resolution. The first variety likely included a wager; the latter, often a jail sentence.

Nevertheless, it was inevitable that the manly art of self-defense would become a respectable pastime, and with it the recognition of those who excelled in the sport. There has never been a shortage of those born in the state or living within its borders who have done exactly that. Observing this, Glenn Feldman, a noted boxing judge and financial planner from Avon, created a sixteen-member committee to help start, along with assistance from Mohegan Sun Casino & Resort and Foxwoods Resort Casino, the Connecticut Boxing Hall of Fame. Forever humble and always quick to note the contributions of others, Feldman began working with his team to choose their inaugural class.

With so many names to choose from, the first inductees, or the class of 2005, were finally selected: Christopher "Bat" Battalino, John Duke, Louis

A view of the impressive wall of inductees inside the Connecticut Boxing Hall of Fame reads like a who's who of both amateur and professional boxing.

"Kid" Kaplan, Willie Pep, Maxie Rosenbloom and Marlon Starling. In a gracious touch, and certainly exemplary of the sensitivity the group prides itself on, they also chose four ancillary awards; Professional Boxer of the Year (Eric Harding), Amateur Boxer of the Year (Tony Grano), Official of the Year (Lou Dell) and Contribution to Boxing Award (Micky Ward).

The Connecticut Boxing Hall of Fame held its first induction ceremony on Thursday evening, December 1, 2005, at Mohegan Sun. Of the three living inductees, only Johnny Duke was able to attend. Honestly speaking, as popular as Duke was with fight fans, not to mention other guests such as Micky Ward, it was probably a good thing. Fans couldn't get enough photos or autographs from both. The interest was high, and the turnout was strong. Not only did the evening have the excitement of a first-time event, but it also drew a plethora of those associated with the sport. The memories came flooding back as each inaugural inductee's name was announced and the moving presentations made it clear that this was indeed destined to become a popular annual event.

In 2006, the event shifted to Foxwoods Resort in Mashantucket, and again it drew considerable attention. More than five hundred tickets were purchased. Names like Bogash, Burns, Leibert, Mann, Ortega and Vejar filled conversations and sparked memories. The mere presence of Manny Leibert, at age ninety-three, was confirmation that the event had now filled the void left behind by the dissolution of the Connecticut Boxing Guild only two years prior. It was Leibert, as many recalled, who had formed the guild back in 1948. Their annual parties at Jacoby's in Meriden became a must-attend event for everyone associated with the sweet science. And like the passing of a boxing title, the guild's belt now belonged to the Connecticut Boxing Hall of Fame.

Next step: a home for the Connecticut Boxing Hall of Fame. But exactly where, when and how? On January 26, 2007, officials from the Mohegan Sun Casino announced that it would serve as the permanent home for the Hall of Fame and that the facility would be located along the concourse of Mohegan Sun Arena. The unveiling of the Connecticut Boxing Hall of Fame took place at the renowned resort on June 12, 2008. Conducting the ribbon-cutting honors were Mohegan Sun senior vice-president of sports and entertainment Paul Munick, Tribal Council chairman Bruce "Two Dogs" Bozsum and Connecticut Boxing Hall of Fame president Glenn Feldman. A twenty-four-foot-long glass display case housed inductee plaques and related boxing memorabilia.

The opening ceremony for the new Connecticut Boxing Hall of Fame inside Mohegan Sun. *From left to right*: Gaspar Ortega, Mike Ortega, Paul Cichon, Kevin "Red Eagle" Brown (background), Micky Ward, Dana Rosenblatt, Glenn Feldman, Kenny Reels and Luigi Camputaro.

By the end of 2016, it was becoming increasingly clear that the popularity and prestige of the Connecticut Boxing Hall of Fame necessitated more space. Once again, Mohegan Sun Casino was there to answer the call. The grand opening of the Hall of Fame's new location in the Casino of the Sky at Mohegan Sun was conducted on June 26, 2017. The well-attended official ribbon-cutting ceremony featured leaders from both the Mashantucket Pequot and Mohegan Tribal Nations, along with John Laudati, president of the Connecticut Boxing Hall of Fame (CBHOF), several board members and celebrity boxers including Micky Ward, Marlon Starling, Gaspar Ortega, Dana Rosenblatt, Troy Wortham, Luigi Camputaro, Orlando Montalvo and Ray Oliveira, to name only a few.

The new CBHOF drew rave reviews and remains open to the public during Mohegan Sun Casino operating hours. In addition to the inductees' plaques and videos of famous fights held in the Nutmeg State, the new location features related boxing memorabilia, along with rotating displays of historically significant events.

"The greatest glory in living lies not in never falling, but in rising every time we fall."
—Nelson Mandela. Gennadiy Golovkin versus Matthew Macklin, MGM Grand at
Foxwoods Resort, June 29, 2013. *Emily Harney / Fightography* ©.

The board of directors for the Connecticut Boxing Hall of Fame (2020) include John Laudati, president; Peter Hary, vice-president; George Phillips, vice-president; Renee Phillips, secretary; Christopher Mund, treasurer; Mike Mazzulli, sergeant at arms; Bob Trieger, publicist; Glenn Feldman, president emeritus; also Mark Allen Baker, Sherman Cain, Johnny Callas, Bill Cholawa, Jason Concepcion, Dick Flaherty, Robin Hayes, Ann Murphy, Kenneth Reels, Chris Renstrom, John Scully, Marlon Starling, Maynard Strickland, Don Trella and Roger Zotti. (Forever inspiring this team are John Burns, Mark Langlais, Manny Leibert, Roland Roy and George Smith, all directors emeritus.)

Ring history has always been written one round at a time. While the rounds belong to the boxers, the minutes between the terms belong to every soul who got them there. They are equally as important and well worth a moment of recall.

CONNECTICUT BOXING HALL OF FAME INDUCTEES AND AWARD WINNERS

Members as of 2019 = 93
* = Member of the Inaugural Class of 2005.

Boxers (49)

Kelvin Anderson	Chad Dawson
Chris "Bat" Battalino	Jack Delaney
Larry Boardman	Sal DiMartino
Lou Bogash	Arturo Gatti
Tyrone Booze	Charles Hadley
Lou Brouillard	Eric Harding
Johnny Callas	Lou "Kid" Kaplan
Luigi Camputaro	Cocoa Kid
Vic Cardell	Julie Kogon
Israel Cardona	Ted Lowry
Johnny Cesario	Carey Mace
Lawrence Clay-Bey	Sean Malone, Jr.
Eddie Compo	Nathan Mann
Dan Cosgrove	Peter Manfredo Jr.
Murray Cain (Teddy Davis)	Orlando Montalvo

Ray Oliveira
Gaspar Ortega
Vinny Paz
Willie Pep
Roland Pier
Bernie Reynolds
Delvin Rodriguez
Dana Rosenblatt
Maxie Rosenbloom
John Ruiz

John Scully
Pinky Silverberg
Travis Simms
Marlon Starling
Gene Tunney
Angel Vazquez
Chico Vejar
Micky Ward
Troy Wortham

Non Participants (38)

Dr. Tony Alessi
Arnie Bayer
Lou Bogash Jr.
F. Mac Buckley
Jimmy Burchfield
John Burns
Paul Cichon
Brian Clark
Desi Clark
George Cruz
Joe DeGuardia
Hugh Devlin
Lou Dibella
Johnny Duke
Glenn Feldman
Shelley Finkel
Dock Flaherty
Bill Gore
John Harris

William Hutt
John "Duke" Lawson
Manny Leibert
Sean Malone Sr.
Arthur Mercante Sr.
Mike Ortega
Daryl Peoples
Kenny Reels
Freddie Roach
Joe Rossi
Roland Roy
George Russo
Clark Sammartino
Dr. Michael Schwartz
Vito Tallarita
Billy Taylor
Peter Timothy
Don Trella
Lou Viscusi

Observers (6)

Al Bernstein
Dan Parker
Mort Sharnik

Bob Steele
Joe Tessitore
Bob Yalen

ANCILLARY AWARDS
2005–19

(a) = amateur

Professional Boxer of the year

2005	Eric Harding
2006–9	Chad Dawson
2010	Matt Remillard
2011	Delvin Rodriguez
2012	Tony Grano
2013	Mike Oliver
2014–15	Luis Rosa
2016	Shelly Vincent
2017	Jimmy Williams
2018	Anthony Laureano
2019	Charles Foster

Amateur Boxer of the Year

2005	Tony Grano
2006	Melissa Roberts
2007	Danny Aquino
2008, 2011	Tramaine Williams
2009	Luis Rosa
2010	Georgie Naclerio
2012	Elvis Figueroa
2013	Mykquan Williams
2014	Izaih Melendez
2015	Chordale Booker
2016	Jacob Marrero
2017	Kevin Bonilla
2018	Nephateria Miller
2019	Felix Parilla

Official(s) of the Year

2005	Lou Dell
2006	George W. Smith
2007, 2015, 2019	Glenn Feldman
2008	George Phillips

2009	Phyllis Roy
2010	Michael Ortega
2011	Don Trella
2012	Dick Flaherty
2013	Lou Pontacoloni (a)
	Bill Maxeiner
2014	Samantha Dane (a)
2014, 2017	Danny Schiavone
2016	Heather Concepcion (a)
	Michael Mazzulli
2017	Sachs Medina (a)
2018	Jason Concepcion (a)
	Peter Hary
2019	Kevin and Roma Smith (a)

Contribution to Boxing

2005	Micky Ward
2006	ESPN 2
2007	Dr. Joseph Carpentieri
2008	Jimmy Burchfield
2009	Paul Cichon
2010	Dr. Michael Schwartz
2011	Peter Timothy
2012	Mitchell Etiss
2013	George Smith
2014	Not awarded
2015	Brian Clark
2016	Carlos Nieves (a)
	Peter Hary Jr.
2017	Hector Rosario
2018	Roland Roy
2019	Sherman Cain

NOTES

Introduction

1. Billed as "Mendoza the Jew," Daniel Mendoza held the title of Champion of England from 1792 to 1795. He was the first prominent Jewish prizefighter in England. Although Mendoza was often smaller than his opponents, he defeated his antagonists with superior technique, speed and agility. His style, known as the Mendoza school, or Jewish school, was credited with inspiring a generation of boxers and with establishing many elements of modern boxing. He would meet Humphries three times, losing only this contest.
2. "Anti-boxing," *Times* (London, Greater London, England), January 9, 1788, 3.

Chapter One

3. Tunney was born on May 25, 1897, at his parent's home at 169 Perry Street in the Greenwich Village section of New York.
4. Tunney was the first and only heavyweight champ to ever do so, until Rocky Marciano joined this exclusive club in 1956.
5. Tunney was introduced to Miss Lauder's older sister, Katherine Dewing, by a longtime friend, Samuel Pryor Jr., who also lived in Greenwich, Connecticut. In turn, Dewing arranged for Tunney and her sister to meet at a dinner party that she and her husband gave at their Manhattan apartment.
6. Previous to his marriage to Mary "Polly" Lauder, Gene Tunney was sued by James Fogarty, charging alienation of his wife's affections, and by Mrs. Katherine King Fogarty for breach of promise. See "Tracing the Black Omen of the Gene Tunney Lost Love Damage Suit," *Ogden Standard-Examiner*, April

5, 1931, 28. The suits were tried in Bridgeport, Connecticut, with Tunney victorious in both. The parasitic tabloids had a field day with the allegations, much to the embarrassment of everyone involved.

Chapter Two

7. "Jack Delaney after Eddie O'Hare's Scalp," *Bridgeport Telegram,* June 17, 1920, 3.
8. "'Solider' Bartfield Wants Five 'Grand' to Box Bogash," *Bridgeport Telegram,* April 15, 1921, 9.
9. Ibid.
10. "Saturday Marks Beginning of Legalized Boxing in the State," *Bridgeport Telegram*, September 28, 1921, 2.
11. "Jack Delaney Wins Decision over Jack McCarron…," *Bridgeport Telegram*, January 28, 1922, 18.
12. "Bogash and Delaney Begin Training…," *Bridgeport Telegram*, January 11, 1922, 5.
13. "Delaney Strips Bogash Of Title," *Hartford Courant*, February 14, 1922, 17.
14. Ibid.

Chapter Three

15. The production of mainly silver, lamps and metal products, glassware, guns and musical instruments attracted craftsmen from all around the globe.
16. "Hanover Park a Delightful Spot," *Hartford Courant,* July 8, 1904, 13.
17. Ibid.
18. "Local Boxing Game Never More Popular," *Hartford Courant*, January 7, 1916, 18.
19. "Waltz Gains the Edge over Shea," *Hartford Courant,* July 22, 1919, 10.
20. Johnny's brothers, Joe "Young" Shugrue and William Shugrue, were also popular Waterbury pugilists.
21. "'Kid' Kaplan Earns Referee's Decision over Johnny Shugrue in Swift Bout at Meriden," *Hartford Courant*, September 15, 1922, 10.
22. Ibid.

Chapter Four

23. "Eight Bouts on Amateur Program," *Hartford Courant*, September 24, 1925.
24. For the record, Battalino refused to meet Mack, who was eight pounds

overweight. Although the pair had been previously matched, they had yet to fight it out. Battalino destroyed Vincent Gullo, who substituted for Mack.

25. Christopher had three brothers (Michael, Palmer and George) and a sister (Mrs. William H. Wilson). There have been numerous spellings and interpretations of his surname.

26. The school was also attended by actor Otis Skinner and singer Sophie Tucker.

27. The Nutmeg Club also worked closely with Hurley in the amateur market.

28. "'Bat' Battalino Knocks Out Holyoke Boy in 1st Round," *Hartford Courant*, July 27, 1926, 14.

29. Some of the shows at the Foot Guard Hall (Armory) were also conducted by the Massasoit Athletic Club.

30. In the semifinal, Battalino knocked out Harry Devine in less than a minute of the opening round.

31. This is the current address for the Capital Grille in Hartford.

32. Hurley Stadium, aka East Hartford Velodrome, was located across the river from downtown, in East Hartford. It was demolished in 1929.

33. Some sources claim that Leto had twelve consecutive victories.

34. The Park River, sometimes called the Hog River, flows through and under the city of Hartford.

35. Lillian arrived in the United States in 1912. The child saved by Battalino was named Louis Casconi.

36. Promoter Hurley was working under his own auspices, "Ed Hurley Boxing Club."

37. As the battle went the full fifteen rounds, Battalino also managed to counter prefight concerns regarding his conditioning.

38. In early 1940, he and his wife, Lillian Rotondo Battalino, lived at 602 Park Road in West Hartford. A friend of his commented that he often recognized Battalino in the gym because he had tattoos on both arms.

Chapter Five

39. There have been incorrect claims of a professional battle(s) prior to this fight against Joey Marcus on July 25, 1940.

Chapter Six

40. Historians are still discovering his bootleg battles.

Chapter Eight

41. Along with Starling were boxers Dan Foley and Daryl Bunkley.
42. Also worth noting during this period, Herb Darity and Steve Hilyard, both talented pugilists, were teammates of Starling. The former grabbed a victory over AAU champion and Golden Gloves champion Dick Eckland of Lowell, Massachusetts.
43. Both boxers were scheduled for four two-minute rounds.

Chapter Nine

44. Maxie Rosenbloom was born on November 1, 1907, at Leonard Bridge (Lebanon), Connecticut. However, he learned to box at Harlem's Union Settlement in New York.
45. This is the current location of the Holiday Inn / Project Management Training Institute.
46. On February 18, 1916, state's attorney Hugh M. Alcorn made it clear that there would be no boxing bouts of any kind in Hartford County. Later, the advent of a state commission would resurrect the sport.
47. Connecticut pugilists have their hometown listed inside the parentheses.
48. Sante's Manor was also a popular Milford ring option.
49. "New Britain News," *Hartford Courant*, October 3, 1914, 13
50. In his eighth professional fight, Willie Pep hit the canvas in the first round of his battle against Carlo Daponde at the Stanley Arena on November 22, 1940. However, Pep won via a sixth-round TKO.
51. In September 1906, "Abe the Newsboy" received a playful tug on his cauliflower ears from President Theodore Roosevelt aboard the presidential yacht USS *Mayflower*. It seems the youngster boarded the boat in an attempt to sell newspapers. Roosevelt, no stranger to the fight game, liked the kid's spunk.
52. Tatta's record was a bit deceiving, as many of those he fought had losing records.

Chapter Ten

53. "Desperate Prize Fight," *New York Herald*, March 3, 1870, 7.
54. Ibid.
55. "Smith-Walcott Fight," *Hartford Courant*, April 15, 1898, 1. Smith forced the fighting during the first half of the battle, but Walcott evened matters in the second half. Attendance was estimated at two thousand.

56. "M'Govern Whipped," *Boston Post*, November 29, 1901, 1.
57. Some sources claim his opponent was Jack McCormick of Philadelphia.
58. Gardner, who had won only one of his last six bouts, avoided Gans and clinched at every opportunity.
59. New York State had an informal leadership role with regard to boxing legislation.
60. "Levinsky Best Bartly Madden in Stirring Bout," *Bridgeport Telegram*, May 28, 1918, 18. Bartley is spelled wrong in the title. Madden was billed as the "logical contender."
61. Due to a detached retina in his right eye that made the eye completely blind, Shugrue had little choice but to retire in 1915. Later, he also suffered from a cataract that left him with only partial vision in the left eye.
62. "Kilbane Stalls in Scrap but Wins over Wallace," *Bridgeport Times and Evening Farmer*, March 27, 1917, 8. Some sources believed that Kilbane's title was on the line.
63. "Greb Slashes Turner in Star Combat," *Bridgeport Telegram*, March 16, 1918, 18. Sources vary with regard to performance assessments.
64. Palitz lost a ten-round newspaper decision to Jack Britton at Church Street Auditorium in Hartford on March 8, 1920, and was defeated by Lou Bogash, via a twelve-round points victory at Casino Hall in Bridgeport on April 26, 1920.
65. Jimmy McLarnin, another elite pugilist, felt that Louis "Kid" Kaplan hit harder than any opponent he had ever faced. Coming from McLarnin, this evaluation speaks volumes.
66. Fantina di Messina, Sicilia, Italy was the birthplace of Luigi Boccasio, aka Lou Bogash.
67. "With Malice Toward None," *Hartford Courant*, March 11, 1978, 78.
68. The Garden AC of Hartford, under Ed Hurley, conducted thirty-eight shows in 1936—nineteen wrestling, sixteen amateur boxing and three professional boxing.
69. Lou Brouillard would vindicate this loss with victories over Gainer on November 23, 1934, and on July 12, 1934.
70. Somewhat motivated by an impending thunderstorm, Al Gainer delivered Barry in forty-eight seconds at Walnut Beach Stadium in Milford.
71. Some documentation notes Herbert's surname as Harwick; numerous variations of his name exist.
72. From 1932 to 1939, Carr compiled an unofficial record of 52-14-8.
73. Regarding his brothers: A lightweight pug who battled from 1943 to 1947, Fred fought primarily out of New England. Fighting from 1944 to 1953, Bobby compiled a record of 72-33-17 while posting victories over Billy Banks, Jimmy Callura and Paul Roach. Incidentally, a few still recall how he managed to last ten rounds against Eddie Compo at the Auditorium in

Hartford on June 8, 1948. In a career spanning five years (1945–50), Henry was a bit unpredictable in the ring; he would win six consecutive battles, then give up two. While the final years of his career were challenging, he did manage a distance loss to elite fighter Jimmy Carter.

74. Boardman lost to elite fighter Tony DeMarco, followed by unanimous decision losses to Johnny Busso and an undefeated Cecil Shorts. The consecutive defeats went the ten-round distance.

75. Brady also sparred with Willie Pep on occasion.

76. Brady compiled an unofficial record of 81-25-6 during a career that spanned from 1944 to 1956.

77. Billy Lynch hung up the gloves in 1963. Some believe that when Robert Cofer discovered his glass chin, during Lynch's first defeat in almost six years, it had something to do with it.

78. Mace pounded Giardello's left eye so bad that the referee had little choice but to stop the fight in the eighth round.

79. The films were *The Midnight Story* (1957) starring Tony Curtis and *World in My Corner* (1956) starring Audie Murphy.

80. Couture was forever known for his $10\frac{1}{2}$-second knockout of Ralph Walton in Lewiston, Maine, on September 24, 1946. It earned him the world record for the quickest knockout in boxing history.

81. By 1977, F. Mac Buckley, state Amateur Athletic Union (AAU) chairman, was talking about having the only club in the United States with weekly amateur boxing. In this case, Marc Antony's nightclub (owned by veteran promoter Frank Maratta).

82. On March 19, 1978, at Veterans Memorial Coliseum in New Haven, Sugar Ray Leonard knocked out Javier Muniz in the opening round of a scheduled eight-round contest. In his previous fight, Muniz had fought ten impressive rounds against Roberto Duran. The fight was televised on ABC's *Wide World of Sports*.

83. Starling retained the WBA welterweight title with a disputed twelve-round draw in a rematch with Mark Breland in 1988. In his battle with Molinares, Starling was knocked out with a punch thrown after the bell had rung to end the sixth round. Although the New Jersey Athletic Control Board later changed the result to a no contest, the WBA didn't reinstate Starling as champion.

Chapter Eleven

84. According to sources, Bonola had nineteen professional fights.

85. Bill Gore handled champions in five different weight divisions.

86. Jimmy Burchfield's Classic Restaurant and Lounge was located at 1058 Charles Street in North Providence.
87. Pete Perone also worked with numerous fight families, including the Balesanos, Berkstroms, LaSalles, Pinkhams and Polowitzers.
88. For greater detail regarding the role of physicians, see Connecticut State Regulations, DUTIES OF COMBAT AREA OFFCIALS, Section 29-143j-39a. Physicians.
89. This document can be accessed online at https://portal.ct.gov//media/DESPP/SLFU/boxing/BoxingMMAregulationsasfiledwiththeSecretaryofStatepdf.pdf?la=en.
90. Please see Section 29-143j-74a. Points, page 28. *State of Connecticut Regulation of the Department of Emergency Services and Public Protection concerning Boxing and Mixed Martial Arts.*
91. Roy Jones (1975–78) was a middleweight from Las Vegas.

Chapter Twelve

92. The fight took place in a bingo hall at the Foxwoods Resort and Casino.
93. The attendance was a bit disappointing at 3,500. For his efforts, Roy Jones Jr. took $2 million back to Pensacola, Florida. It was an interesting battle despite the relatively few punches that were thrown.
94. Freitas was deducted a point in the tenth round for a low blow.
95. Before the contest even began, controversy surfaced when both fighters objected to their opponent's hand wraps.
96. During the remainder of the contest, Holiday's corner managed to control a gash on the fighter's right eye that occurred during the seventh round.
97. Toney versus McCallum I ended in draw, while James Toney picked up a majority-decision victory in their second battle. An accurate right by Toney sliced the right eye of McCallum in the eighth round.
98. The fight waned a bit in the seventh round for lack of engagement. Mosley rode the bike.
99. Lewis, in his fourth title defense, in actuality didn't ignite until the fourth round. This was Mavrovic's last fight. Referee Frank Cappuccino, noticeably smaller, was slow at asserting his commands.
100. Ironically, in his win over Hasim Rahman on November 6, 1999, Maskaev sent Rahman out of the ring in the same manner; Johnson was stripped of the title on February 22, 2001, for failure to defend.
101. Mark Johnson was eight years older than Fernando Montiel.
102. Fernando Montiel, in a lackluster performance, in point of fact didn't begin engaging until the eighth round.

103. The title was stripped from Marcos Ramirez for failure to defend.
104. Television replays confirmed the misfire as going south.
105. Malignaggi developed a cut on the left eyelid during the fifth round.
106. Vera had opened a cut above Lee's right eye in the fourth round.
107. Echols was in truth pushed away from Brewer by Ortega, while the referee called a knockdown of Brewer, who was on the ropes.

BIBLIOGRAPHY

Books

Baker, Mark Allen. *Battling Nelson, the Durable Dane*. Jefferson, NC: McFarland & Company, 2016.

———. *Between the Ropes at Madison Square Garden: The History of an Iconic Boxing Ring, 1925–2007*. Jefferson, NC: McFarland & Company, 2019

———. *The Fighting Times of Abe Attell*. Jefferson, NC: McFarland & Company, 2017.

———. *Title Town USA: Boxing in Upstate New York*. Charleston, SC: The History Press, 2010.

———. *The World Colored Heavyweight Championship, 1876–1937*. Jefferson, NC: McFarland & Company, 2012.

Cavanaugh, Jack. *Tunney: Boxing's Brainiest Champ and His Upset of the Great Jack Dempsey*. New York: Ballantine Books, 2006.

Goldman, Herbert G., ed. The Ring *Record Book and Boxing Encyclopedia*. New York: Ring Publishing, 1985.

———. *Boxing, A Worldwide Record of Bouts and Boxers*. Jefferson, NC: McFarland & Company, 2012.

Kahn, Roger. *A Flame of Pure Fire: Jack Dempsey and the Roaring '20s*. New York: Harcourt, Brace & Company, 1999.

Sugar, Bert Randolph. *Boxing's Greatest Fighters*. Guilford, CT: Lyons Press, 2006.

———. *The Ultimate Book of Boxing Lists*. Philadelphia: Running Press, 2010.

Archival Sources

Connecticut Boxing Hall of Fame
Foxwoods Resort and Casino
International Boxing Hall of Fame
Library of Congress
Mohegan Sun Casino & Resort

Articles and Blog Entries

Cain, Sherman. "Johnny Duke Fought the Good Fight." *Journal Inquirer*. March 8, 2006
_____."A Match with Fame, Enfield's Tallarita Among State Boxing Hall's Class of '09." *Journal Inquirer*. September 11, 2009.

Brochures and Programs

Annual Induction Ceremony, Connecticut Boxing Guild, 1948–2004.
Annual Induction Ceremony, Connecticut Boxing Hall of Fame, 2005–present.
Annual Induction Ceremony, International Boxing Hall of Fame, various years.

Internet Sites

Box Rec. boxrec.com.
Britannica. britannica.com.
Charter Oak Boxing Academy. cobaboxing.net.
Cyber Boxing Zone. cyberboxingzone.com.
ESPN. espn.com.
Find a Grave. findagrave.com.
History.com. history.com.
International Boxing Hall of Fame. ibhof.com.
JO Sports. josportsinc.com.
Newspapers.com newspapers.com.
Tha Boxing Voice. thaboxingvoice.com.
Wikipedia. wikipedia.org.
YouTube. youtube.com.

Legal Source

Connecticut State Regulations, Hartford, Connecticut

Magazines

Boxing Monthly
Boxing News
Boxing Scene
KO
Police Gazette
Sporting News
Sports Illustrated
The Ring
USA Boxing News
Weekly Boxing World

Newspapers

Atlanta Constitution
Arizona Republic (Phoenix)
Baltimore Sun
Bennington (VT) Banner
Boston Globe
Boston Post
Bridgeport (CT) Telegram
Bridgeport (CT) Times and Evening Farmer
Brooklyn Citizen
Brooklyn Daily Eagle
Calexico (CA) Chronicle
Chicago Tribune
Cincinnati Enquirer
Connecticut Post (Bridgeport)
Courier-News (Bridgewater, NJ)
Courier-Post (Camden, NJ)
Daily News (New York)
Danbury (CT) News-Times
The Day (New London, CT)
Hartford Courant

BIBLIOGRAPHY

Journal Inquirer (Manchester, CT)
Meriden (CT) Record-Journal
New Britain (CT) Herald
New Haven Register
New York Herald
New York Times
Norwalk (CT) Hour
Ogden (UT) Standard-Examiner
Republican-American (Waterbury, CT)
Stamford (CT) Advocate

Organizations

Bureau of Labor Statistics' Consumer Price Index (CPI)
Connecticut Boxing Guild
Connecticut Boxing Hall of Fame
International Boxing Hall of Fame
International Boxing Research Organization: IBRO
The Smithsonian Institution
United States Census Bureau

Trademarks

CLETO REYES is a registered trademark of Industria Reyes S.A. de C.V.
Connecticut Boxing Hall of Fame is a registered 501(c)(3) nonprofit organization.
Everlast logo is a registered trademark of Active Apparel Group (AAGP).
FOXWOODS is a trade name and service mark of the Mashantucket Pequot Tribe.
KRONK logo is a registered trademark of Second Round Incorporated.
Main Events logo is a registered trademark of New Jersey Sports Productions Incorporated.
Mohegan Sun logo is a registered trademark of Mohegan Gaming & Entertainment (MGE), a master developer and operator of premier global integrated entertainment resorts, including Mohegan Sun in Uncasville, Connecticut.
WBC logo is a registered trademark of World Boxing Council.

ABOUT THE AUTHOR

Mark Allen Baker is a former business executive, author, biographer and writer of hundreds of articles and over twenty-five nonfiction books. He is the only person to serve the International Boxing Hall of Fame as an author, historian, chairperson, sponsor, volunteer and biographer. He is also on the board of directors of the Connecticut Boxing Hall of Fame. A graduate of the State University of New York, his expertise has been referenced in numerous periodicals, including *USA Today*, *Sports Illustrated* and *Money* magazine.

Visit us at
www.historypress.com